THE LITTLE
BOOK *of*
PRAYERS

Edited by
DAVID SCHILLER

WORKMAN PUBLISHING • NEW YORK

Library of Congress Cataloging-in-Publication Data

The little book of prayers/[edited] by David Schiller.
p.   cm
ISBN 0-7611-0453-4
1. Prayers.   I. Schiller, David.
BL560.L584   1996
291.4'3—dc20   96-10866
                                            CIP

Workman books are available at special discounts when purchased in bulk for
premiums and sales promotions as well as for fundraising or educational use.
Special editions can also be created to specification. For details, contact the
Special Sales Director at the address below.

Workman Publishing Company, Inc.
708 Broadway, New York, NY 10003-9555

Manufactured in the United States of America
First Printing October 1996

16 15 14 13 12 11 10

FOR THEO AND QUINN

———◆———

With special thanks to
Bill Carr, Rachel Ravitz, Matthew Brown;
Paul, Jim, Ruth, Diane, and Peter;
and to Asa, as ever.

The Little Book of Prayers is an anthology of prayers from around the world. Some prayers will be familiar, many not. The book is not intended to be comprehensive. Prayers are arranged in mood from "light" to "dark" or morning to night, and also by the serendipity of choice. An index and a selective guide are provided in the back to help the reader locate prayers by author and tradition, and by theme, occasion or need.

INTRODUCTION

Prayer oneth the soul to God.

*H*ow soon after humans stood upright and turned to the sky did they begin to pray? When did the first person watch the sun rise and lift his heart in praise? Or stand over a sick child and ask "Why?" It must have been immediate; prayer seems almost as natural as breathing. In editing a collection of prayers this is the first thing one understands—prayer, like music or poetry, is everywhere in the world. Its impulse is universal. And whether it is the Christian's "Our Father" or a Navajo chant to the Lord of the Mountains, the truths expressed in this impulse are universal, too.

We pray to give thanks. We pray to ask for answers. We pray to receive, pray to give. We very much pray for help. We pray before we eat. And before we sleep we ask "the Lord our souls to keep," to paraphrase the 12th-century prayer known by so many Western children. There are names for different types of prayer—praise, petition, thanksgiving and atonement are some. But we don't need to understand the terms to understand the soul's cry, or the beautiful language crafted to express it.

There is another universal quality to prayer, and that is humility. The Muslim surrenders. The Christian mystic prays to fold herself into the Lord. "Bow, stubborn knees!" says Hamlet. Even Jesus prayed, "Not what I will, but what thou wilt." Whether our prayer is to a God, a godhead, a spirit or a tree, we can approach, literally or figuratively, only on our knees. Ego and arrogance have no place in prayer.

And in an age that could be characterized by its astonishing lack of humility, prayer offers a rare chance to put our inflated selves aside, and in the suddenly unburdened state that follows rediscover the things that really matter. Which is perhaps why, living in the age that we do, we are also just beginning to rediscover the need for prayer.

Arise, you little glancing wings
  & sing your infant joy!
Arise & drink your bliss!
For every thing that lives is holy;
  for the source of life
Descends to be a weeping babe;
For the Earthworm renews the
  moisture of the sandy plain.

—WILLIAM BLAKE
"Vala, or The Four Zoas"

The light of God surrounds me;
The love of God enfolds me;
The power of God protects me;
The presence of God watches over
    me.
Wherever I am, God is.

—JAMES DILLET FREEMAN
"Prayer of Protection"

I shall sing a praise to God:
Strike the chords upon the drum.
God who gives us all good things—
Strike the chords upon the drum—
Wives, and wealth, and wisdom.
Strike the chords upon the drum.

—PRAYER FROM ZAIRE

Praise ye the LORD. Praise ye the LORD from the
heavens: praise him in the heights.

Praise ye him, all his angels: praise ye him, all his
hosts.

Praise ye him, sun and moon: praise him, all ye stars
of light.

Praise him, ye heavens of heavens, and ye waters
that be above the heavens.

Let them praise the name of the LORD: for he
commanded, and they were created.

He hath also stablished them for ever and ever: he
hath made a decree which shall not pass.

Praise the LORD from the earth, ye dragons, and all
deeps:

Fire, and hail; snow, and vapours; stormy wind
    fulfilling his word:
Mountains, and all hills; fruitful trees, and all cedars;
Beasts, and all cattle; creeping things, and flying
    fowl:
Kings of the earth, and all people; princes, and all
    judges of the earth:
Both young men, and maidens; old men, and
    children:
Let them praise the name of the LORD: for his name
    alone is excellent; his glory is above the earth and
      heaven.
He also exalteth the horn of his people, the praise of
    all his saints; even of the children of Israel, a
      people near unto him. Praise ye the LORD.

—PSALM 148

$\mathcal{W}$e will sing thy praises, O God almighty. We will now and evermore sing thy praises, even as they were sung of old. For thy laws are immutable, O God: they are firm like the mountains.

—THE VEDAS

*Y*ou are the notes, and we are the flute.
We are the mountain, you are the sounds
    coming down.
We are the pawns and kings and rooks
you set out on a board: we win or we lose.
We are lions rolling and unrolling on flags.
Your invisible wind carries us through the
    world.

—JELALUDDIN RUMI

The earth has been laid down, the earth has
  been laid down
The earth has been laid down, it has been
  made,
The earth spirit has been laid down
It is covered over with growing things, it has
  been laid down.
The earth has been laid down, it has been
  made.
The sky has been set up, the sky has been set
  up
The sky has been set up, it has been made.

The mountains have been laid down, the
mountains have been laid down
The mountains have been laid down, they have
been made.
The waters have been laid down, the waters
have been laid down
The waters have been laid down, they have
been made.
The clouds have been set up, the clouds have
been set up
The clouds have been set up, they have been
made.

—NAVAJO SWEATHOUSE CHANT

Wherever I go—only
Thou! Wherever I stand—only
Thou! Just Thou, again Thou!
always Thou! Thou, Thou,
Thou! When things are good,
Thou! when things are bad—
Thou! Thou, Thou, Thou!

—HASIDIC SONG

The prayer preceding all prayers is "May it be the real I who speaks. May it be the real Thou that I speak to."

—C.S. LEWIS

*B*lessed art Thou, Lord our God, King of the universe, who forms light and creates darkness, who makes peace and creates all things.

Who mercifully sheds light upon the earth and upon all who dwell on it.

And who in His goodness, renews the works of creation every day continually.

"How many are Thy works O Lord, in wisdom hast Thou made them all, the earth is filled with Thy creations!"

Blessed art Thou, Lord our God, King of the universe, who with His word brings on the evenings,

With wisdom opens the gates,

With understanding alters the phases, varies the seasons,

And arranges the stars in their heavenly orbit
according to His will.
He creates day and night.
He rolls away the light from before the darkness and
the darkness from before the light,
He makes the day to pass and the night to come, and
divides between day and night;
Lord of hosts in His name.
A living and everlasting God, who shall constantly
reign over us forever and ever.
Blessed art Thou, Lord, who brings on the evenings.

—JEWISH EVENING BLESSING
"Birkat Maariv"

*I*n the Name of God, the merciful Lord of
  mercy.
Praise be to God, the Lord of all being,
the merciful Lord of mercy,
Master of the day of judgment.
You alone we serve: to You alone we come for
  aid.
Guide us in the straight path,
the path of those whom You have blessed,
not of those against whom there is displeasure,
nor of those who go astray.

—THE KORAN
"Opener Prayer"

$\mathcal{B}$e a gardener.
Dig a ditch,
toil and sweat,
and turn the earth upside down
and seek the deepness
and water the plants in time.
Continue this labor
and make sweet floods to run
and noble and abundant fruits to spring.
Take this food and drink
and carry it to God
as your true worship.

—JULIAN OF NORWICH

*A*ll you big things, bless the Lord
Mount Kilimanjaro and Lake Victoria
The Rift Valley and the Serengeti Plain
Fat baobabs and shady mango trees
All eucalyptus and tamarind trees
Bless the Lord
Praise and extol Him for ever and ever

All you tiny things, bless the Lord
Busy black ants and hopping fleas
Wriggling tadpoles and mosquito larvae
Flying locusts and water drops
Pollen dust and tsetse flies
Millet seeds and dried dagaa
Bless the Lord
Praise and extol Him for ever and ever.

—EAST AFRICAN CANTICLE

I believe a leaf of grass is no less
   than the journey-work of the
      stars,
And the pismire is equally perfect,
   and a grain of sand, and the egg
      of the wren,
And the tree-toad is a chef-d'oeuvre
   for the highest,
And the running blackberry would
   adorn the parlors of heaven,

And the narrowest hinge in my
 hand puts to scorn all
  machinery,
And the cow crunching with
 depress'd head surpasses any
  statue,
And a mouse is miracle enough to
 stagger sextillions of infidels.

—WALT WHITMAN

*M*ake a joyful noise unto the LORD, all ye
   lands.
Serve the LORD with gladness: come before his
   presence with singing.
Know ye that the LORD he is God: it is he that
   hath made us, and not we ourselves; we are
   his people, and the sheep of his pasture.
Enter into his gates with thanksgiving, and into
   his courts with praise: be thankful unto him,
   and bless his name.
For the LORD is good; his mercy is everlasting;
   and his truth endureth to all generations.

—PSALM 100

With your feet I walk
I walk with your limbs
I carry forth your body
For me your mind thinks
Your voice speaks for me
Beauty is before me
And beauty is behind me
Above and below me hovers the beautiful
I am surrounded by it
I am immersed in it
In my youth I am aware of it
And in old age I shall walk quietly
The beautiful trail.

—NAVAJO PRAYER

The lark's on the wing;
The snail's on the thorn:
God's in his Heaven—
All's right with the world!

—ROBERT BROWNING

Bless Thee, O Lord, for the living arc of the sky
over me this morning.

Bless Thee, O Lord, for the companionship of night
mist far above the skyscraper peaks I saw when I
woke once during the night.

Bless Thee, O Lord, for the miracle of light to my
eyes and the mystery of it ever changing.

Bless Thee, O Lord, for the laws Thou hast ordained
holding fast these tall oblongs of stone and steel,
holding fast the planet Earth in its course and
farther beyond the cycle of the Sun.

—CARL SANDBURG

All Creation rejoices in you,
O Full of Grace,
The archangels and the race of men,
O Sanctified Temple and Spiritual
Paradise, the Glory of Virgins;
From whom God was incarnate
and became a child, our God
throughout the ages.
He made your body into a throne.
And your womb he made more
spacious than the heavens.
All creation rejoices in you,
O Full of Grace, glory to you!

—EASTERN ORTHODOX LITURGY

*M*y praise dispraises Thee,
   Almighty God,
For praise is being and to be
   is sin.

—SUFI PRAYER

My God, I love you.

—St. Thérèse of Lisieux
on Her Deathbed

Prayer is man's conversation with God. It is the most secret and intimate relationship which man can enter into with the Lord of the Universe. He speaks with God as 'thou' from a sense of innermost closeness and tells Him everything which troubles, moves and makes him happy. His prayer may be improvised or he may use an age-old form, a cliché sanctified by a hundred generations and which has become meaningful for man. He may say his prayer aloud, chant it, whisper it or keep it in the recesses of his heart.

—VLADIMIR LINDENBERG

Keep me as the apple of
    the eye,
hide me under the shadow
    of thy wings.

—PSALM 17:8

You, O eternal Trinity, are a deep sea into which, the more I enter, the more I find, and the more I find, the more I seek.

   O abyss,
      O eternal Godhead,
         O sea profound,
what more could you give me than yourself?
Amen.

—St. Catherine of Siena

*L*ord, you are my lover,
My longing,
My flowing stream,
My sun,
And I am your reflection.

—MECHTHILD OF MAGDEBURG

O nectar! O delicious stream!
O ravishing and only pleasure! Where
    Shall such another theme
Inspire my tongue with joys, or please mine ear!
    Abridgment of delights!
        And queen of sights!
O mine of rarities! O kingdom wide!
O more! O cause of all! O glorious bride!
    O God! O bride of God! O king!
    O soul and crown of everything!

—THOMAS TRAHERNE

𝓑less the Lord, sun and moon, sing praise
    to him and highly exalt him for ever.
Bless the Lord, stars of heaven.
Bless the Lord, all rain and dew.
Bless the Lord, all winds.
Bless the Lord, fire and heat.
Bless the Lord, winter cold and summer heat.
Bless the Lord, dews and snows.
Bless the Lord, nights and days.
Bless the Lord, light and darkness.
Bless the Lord, ice and cold.
Bless the Lord, frosts and snows.
Bless the Lord, lightnings and clouds.

Let the earth bless the Lord; let it sing praise to
     him and highly exalt him for ever.
Bless the Lord, mountains and hills.
Bless the Lord, all things that grow on the
     earth.
Bless the Lord, you springs.
Bless the Lord, seas and rivers.
Bless the Lord, you whales and all creatures
     that move in the waters.
Bless the Lord, all birds of the air.
Bless the Lord, all beasts and cattle, sing praise
     to him and highly exalt him for ever.

—SONG OF THE THREE YOUNG MEN

*L*ord, we brought in the harvest.
The rain watered the earth,
the sun drew cassava and corn out of the
clay. Your mercy showered blessing after
blessing over our country. Creeks grew into
rivers; swamps became lakes. Healthy fat
cows gaze on the green sea of the savanna.
The rain smoothed out the clay walls, the
mosquitoes drowned in the high waters.

Lord, the yam is fat like meat,
    the cassava melts on the tongue, oranges
    burst in their peels, dazzling and bright.

Lord, nature gives thanks,
    Your creatures give thanks. Your praise rises
    in us like the great river.

—WEST AFRICAN PRAYER

Praise God, from whom all
  blessings flow!
Praise Him, all creatures here
  below!
Praise Him above, ye heavenly
  host!
Praise Father, Son, and Holy Ghost!

—THOMAS KEN

For your sake I said I will praise the moon,
tell the colour of the river,
find new words for the agony
and ecstasy of gulls.

Because you are close,
everything that men make, observe
or plant is close, is mine:
the gulls slowly writhing, slowly singing
on the spears of wind;
the iron gate above the river;
the bridge holding between stone fingers
her cold bright necklace of pearls.

—LEONARD COHEN
"Owning Everything"

We praise Thee, O God, for Thy glory
displayed in all the creatures of the earth.
They affirm Thee in living; all things affirm
Thee in living; the bird in the air, both the
hawk and the finch; the beast on the earth,
both the wolf and the lamb; the worm in the
soil and the worm in the belly.
Therefore man, whom Thou hast made to be
conscious of Thee, must consciously praise
Thee, in thought and in word and in deed.

Even with the hand to the broom, the back bent
    in laying the fire, the knee bent in cleaning
    the hearth, we, the scrubbers and sweepers of
    Canterbury,
The back bent under toil, the knee bent under
    sin, the hands to the face under fear, the head
    bent under grief,
Even in us the voices of seasons, the snuffle of
    winter, the song of spring, the drone of
    summer, the voices of beasts and of birds,
    praise Thee.

—T.S. ELIOT
Murder in The Cathedral

How wonderful, O Lord, are the works of your
 hands!
The heavens declare Your glory,
the arch of sky displays Your handiwork.
In Your love You have given us the power
to behold the beauty of Your world
robed in all its splendor.
The sun and the stars, the valleys and hills,
the rivers and lakes all disclose Your presence.

The roaring breakers of the sea tell of
    Your awesome might;
the beasts of the field and the birds of the air
bespeak Your wondrous will.
In Your goodness You have made us able to hear
the music of the world. The voices of loved ones
reveal to us that You are in our midst.
A divine voice sings through all creation.

—ADAPTATION OF PSALM 104

To him with trumpets and with
  flutes,
With cornets, clarions, and with
  lutes,
With harps, with organs, and with
  shawms,
With holy anthems and with psalms,
With voice of angels and of men,
Sing Alleluia: amen, amen.

—JOHN DAVIES

$\mathcal{P}$rayer is
The world in tune,
A spirit-voice,
And vocal joys
Whose *echo* is heaven's bliss.

—HENRY VAUGHAN

Father of night, Father of day,
Father, who taketh the darkness away,
Father, who teacheth the bird to fly,
Builder of rainbows up in the sky,
Father of loneliness and pain,
Father of love and Father of rain.

Father of day, Father of night,
Father of black, Father of white,
Father, who build the mountain so high,
Who shapeth the cloud up in the sky,
Father of time, Father of dreams,
Father, who turneth the rivers and streams.

Father of grain, Father of wheat,
Father of cold and Father of heat,
Father of air and Father of trees,
Who dwells in our hearts and our memories,
Father of minutes, Father of days,
Father of whom we most solemnly praise.

—BOB DYLAN
"Father of Night"

I am bending my knee,
In the eye of the Father who
    created me,
In the eye of the Son who
    purchased me,
In the eye of the Spirit who
    cleansed me,
In friendship and affection.

—CELTIC RUNE

Hail, holy queen,
mother of mercy, our life, our sweetness, and our
    hope.
To thee do we cry, poor banished children of Eve.
To thee do we send up our sighs
Mourning and weeping in this vale of tears.
Turn then, most gracious advocate,
Thine eyes of mercy toward us,
And after this exile
Show us the blessed fruit of thy womb, Jesus.
O clement, O loving, O sweet Virgin Mary.

Pray for us, O Holy Mother of God,
That we may be made worthy of the promises of
    Christ.

—PRAYER TO MARY
"Salve Regina"

Praise be to him who alone is to be praised. Praise him for his grace and favour. Praise him for his power and goodness. Praise him whose knowledge encompasses all things.

O God, grant me light in my heart and light in my tomb, light in my hearing and light in my seeing, light in my flesh, light in my blood and light in my bones.

Light before me, light behind me, light to right of me, light to left of me, light above me, light beneath me.

O God, increase my light and give me the greatest light of all. Of thy mercy grant me light, O thou most merciful.

—ABU HAMID AL-GHAZALI

$\mathcal{G}$lory be to God for dappled things—
   For skies of couple-colour as a brinded cow;
      For rose-moles all in stipple upon trout that
         swim;
Fresh-firecoal chestnut falls; finches' wings;
   Landscape plotted and pieced—fold, fallow, and
      plough;
      And all trades, their gear and tackle and trim.
All things counter, original, spare, strange;
   Whatever is fickle, freckled (who knows how?)
      With swift, slow; sweet, sour; adazzle, dim;
He fathers-forth whose beauty is past change:
      Praise him.

—GERARD MANLEY HOPKINS
"Pied Beauty"

*H*e who is in the sun, and in the fire and in the heart of man is ONE. He who knows this is one with the ONE.

—THE UPANISHADS

Our Father which art in heaven,
Hallowed be thy name.
Thy kingdom come. Thy will be done in earth,
as it is in heaven.
Give us this day our daily bread.
And forgive us our debts, as we forgive our
debtors.
And lead us not into temptation, but deliver us
from evil:
For thine is the kingdom, and the power, and
the glory, for ever.
Amen.

—MATTHEW 6:9–13

The Our Father contains all possible petitions; we cannot conceive of any prayer not already contained in it. It is to prayer what Christ is to humanity. It is impossible to say once through, giving the fullest possible attention to each word, without a change, infinitesimal perhaps but real, taking place in the soul.

—SIMONE WEIL

O God, O lord of the mountains and valleys, I have offered you a bit of your food, your drink. And now I continue on, beneath your feet and your hands, I, a traveler.

Now I will sleep beneath your feet, beneath your hands, O lord of the mountains and valleys, O lord of the trees, O lord of the creeping vines. Again tomorrow there will be day, again tomorrow there will be light. I know not where I will be.

Who is my mother? Who is my father? Only you, O God. You watch me, guard me, on every path, through every darkness, and before each obstacle that you might hide or take away, O God, my lord, O lord of the mountains and valleys.

—KEKCHI MAYA

We rose before dawn
to praise you,
bringing our song to your Lotus
   Feet—
hear what we ask!
Please listen,
you who were born among us
into this cowherding clan—
What choice do you have
but to take us into your service,
your heartfelt servants, your kin?

We didn't come to receive the outer
   drum,
the drum of a day, O Govinda—
We are yours for life.
Make all our desires be for you,
it is you alone that we want. Hear
   our song!

—ANTAL

*M*y heart lies before you, O my God. Look deep within. See these memories of mine, for you are my hope. You cleanse me when unclean humours such as these possess me, by drawing my eyes to yourself and saving my feet from the snare.

—ST. AUGUSTINE

Oh my Lord,

If I worship you
from the fear of hell, burn me in hell.

If I worship you
from the hope of Paradise, bar me from
        its gates.

But if I worship you
for yourself alone, grant me the beauty
        of your Face.

—RABI'A

*W*hy should I call Thee Lord, Who art my
    God?
    Why should I call Thee Friend, Who art my
        Love?
    Or King, Who art my very Spouse above?
Or call Thy Sceptre on my heart Thy rod?
    Lo now Thy banner over me is love,
All heaven flies open to me at Thy nod:
For Thou hast lit Thy flame in me a clod,
    Made me a nest for dwelling of Thy Dove.
    What wilt Thou call me in our home above,

Who now has called me friend? how will it be
　　When Thou for good wine settest forth the
　　　　best?
Now Thou dost bid me come and sup with
　　Thee,
　　Now Thou dost make me lean upon Thy
　　　　breast:
　　How will it be with me in time of Love?

—CHRISTINA ROSSETTI
"After Communion"

This world,
　　compared to You—

a lake so tiny
　　even a mustard seed
　　is too large for it to hold.

Yet from the lake all Beings drink.

And into it deer, jackals,
  rhinoceri, sea-elephants falling.

From the earliest moment of birth,
  falling and falling in You.

—LAL DED

I find you, Lord, in all Things
and in all
my fellow creatures, pulsing with
your life;
as a tiny seed you sleep in what is
small
and in the vast you vastly yield
yourself.

—RAINER MARIA RILKE
The Book of Hours

When I am liberated by silence, when I am no longer involved in the measurement of life, but in the living of it, I can discover a form of prayer in which there is effectively no distraction. My whole life becomes a prayer. My whole silence is full of prayer. The world of silence in which I am immersed contributes to my prayer.

—THOMAS MERTON

$\mathcal{G}$lorious Lord, I give you greeting!
Let the church and the chancel praise you.
Let the chancel and the church praise you.
Let the plain and the hillside praise you.
Let the world's three well-springs praise you.
Two above wind and one above land,
Let the dark and the daylight praise you.
Abraham, founder of the faith, praised you:
Let the life everlasting praise you.
Let the birds and honeybees praise you,
Let the shorn stems and the shoots praise you.
Both Aaron and Moses praised you:
Let the male and the female praise you,

Let the seven days and the stars praise you,
Let the air and the ether praise you,
Let the books and the letters praise you,
Let the fish in the swift streams praise you,
Let the thought and the action praise you,
Let the sand-grains and the earth-clods praise
    you,
Let all the good that's performed praise you.
And I shall praise you, Lord of glory:
Glorious Lord, I give you greeting!

—GAELIC BENEDICTION

It is lovely indeed, it is lovely indeed.
I, I am the spirit within the earth . . .
The feet of the earth are my feet . . .
The legs of the earth are my legs . . .
The bodily strength of the earth is my strength . . .
The thoughts of the earth are my thoughts . . .
The voice of the earth is my voice . . .
The feather of the earth is my feather . . .
All that belongs to the earth belongs to me . . .
All that surrounds the earth surrounds me . . .
I, I am the sacred words of the earth . . .
It is lovely indeed, it is lovely indeed.

—Navajo Song

*H*eaven is His head
Earth His feet.
Four compass points are His hands.
Sun and moon are His eyes.
Ether is His breath.
Fire is His mouth.
Teaching is His breast.
Non-teaching is His back.
Grass and plants are His hair.
Mountains are His bones.
Sea is His bladder.
Rivers are His veins.

—LAURETANIAN LITANY

I will be truthful.

I will suffer no injustice.

I will be free from fear.

I will not use force.

I will be of good will to all
men.

—MAHATMA GANDHI

Christ with me, Christ before me, Christ
   behind me,
Christ in me, Christ beneath me, Christ above
   me,
Christ on my right, Christ on my left,
Christ when I lie down, Christ when I sit down,
   Christ when I arise,
Christ in the heart of everyone who thinks of me,
Christ in the mouth of everyone who speaks of
   me,
Christ in every eye that sees me,
Christ in every ear that hears me.

—ST. PATRICK

*I*t is right, O God, that peoples sing thy praises, and that they are glad and rejoice in thee. All evil spirits fly away in fear; but the hosts of the saints bow down before thee.

How could they not bow down in love and adoration, before thee, God of gods, Spirit Supreme? Thou creator of Brahma, the god of creation, thou infinite, eternal, refuge of the world! Thou who art all that is, and all that is not, and all that is Beyond.

Thou God from the beginning, God in man since man was. Thou Treasure supreme of this vast universe. Thou the One to be known and the Knower, the final resting place. Thou Infinite Presence in whom all things are.

———◆———

Adoration unto thee who art before me and behind me: adoration unto thee who art on all sides, God of all. All-powerful God of immeasurable might. Thou art the consummation of all: thou art all.

—THE BHAGAVAD GITA

Glory to you for the feast-day of life.
Glory to you for the perfume of lilies and roses.
Glory to you for each different taste of berry
  and fruit.
Glory to you for the sparkling silver of early
  morning dew.
Glory to you for the joy of dawn's awakening.
Glory to you for the new life each day brings.

—GREGORY PETROV

Waking up this morning, I
   smile.
Twenty-four brand new hours are
   before me.
I vow to live fully in each moment
   and to look at all beings with
   eyes of compassion.

—THICH NHAT HANH

Therefore the limbs You have planted in us,
The spirit You have infused within us,
The tongue You have put in our mouths—
They shall all thankfully acknowledge, bless,
praise, laud, exalt,
    glorify, sanctify, and proclaim Your
sovereignty, O our king.
For every mouth shall acknowledge You,
Every tongue shall pledge loyalty to You,
Every knee shall bend to You,
Every back shall bow to You,
Every heart shall revere You,
Every inward part shall sing unto Your name—

As it is written:
    All my bones shall say,
       "Lord, who is like You?
       You save the poor from one stronger than
          he, the poor
    and needy from his despoiler" (Ps. 35:10).

                         —SABBATH MORNING PRAYER

*M*y life is an instant,
a fleeting hour.
My life is a moment,
which swiftly escapes me.
O my God, you know that
on earth I have only today
to love you.

—St. Thérèse of Lisieux

Sometimes there is an expression of an almost physical longing to experience the presence of God, without whom life seems to have little meaning: "God, You are my God; I search for You, my soul thirsts for You, my body yearns for You" (Ps. 63:2).

—Reuven Hammer

Unbreakable, O Lord,
Is the love
That binds me to You:
Like a diamond,
It breaks the hammer that strikes it.

My heart goes into You
As the polish goes into the gold.
As the lotus lives in its water,
I live in You.

Like the bird
That gazes all night
At the passing moon,
I have lost myself dwelling in You.

O my Beloved—
Return.

—MIRABAI

I pray not for wealth, I pray not for honours, I pray not for pleasures, or even the joys of poetry. I only pray that during all my life I may have love: that I may have pure love to love Thee.

—CHAITANYA

O love, O pure deep love, be here,
   be now
Be all; worlds dissolve into your
   stainless endless radiance,
Frail living leaves burn with you
   brighter than cold stars:
Make me your servant, your breath,
   your core.

—JELALUDDIN RUMI

love is not concerned
with whom you pray
or where you slept
the night you ran away
from home
love is concerned
that the beauty of your heart
should kill no one.

—ALICE WALKER
"Love Is Not Concerned"

*G*od help us to live slowly:

To move simply:

To look softly:

To allow emptiness:

To let the heart create for us.

Amen.

—MICHAEL LEUNIG

O world, I cannot hold thee close enough!
　　Thy winds, thy wide grey skies!
　　Thy mists, that roll and rise!
Thy woods, this autumn day, that ache and sag
And all but cry with colour! That gaunt crag
To crush! To lift the lean of that black bluff!
World, World, I cannot get thee close enough!

Long have I known a glory in it all,
   But never knew I this:
   Here such a passion is
As stretcheth me apart,—Lord, I do fear
Thou'st made the world too beautiful this year;
My soul is all but out of me,—let fall
No burning leaf; prithee, let no bird call.

—EDNA ST. VINCENT MILLAY
"God's World"

...elter—
My Friend—
My Food for the Journey—
My Journey's End—
You are my breath,
My hope,
My companion,
My craving,
My abundant wealth.
Without You—my Life, my Love—

I would never have wandered across these
    endless countries.
You have poured out so much grace for me,
Done me so many favors, given me so many
    gifts—
I look everywhere for Your love—
Then suddenly I am filled with it.
O Captain of my Heart,
Radiant Eye of Yearning in my breast,
I will never be free from You
As long as I live.
Be satisfied with me, Love
And I am satisfied.

—RABI'A

*W*ouldest thou wit thy Lord's meaning in this thing? Wit it well: Love was his meaning. Who shewed it thee? Love. What shewed He thee? Love. Wherefore shewed it He? for Love . . . Thus was I learned that Love is our Lord's meaning.

—JULIAN OF NORWICH

*M*y soul doth magnify the Lord,
And my spirit hath rejoiced in God my Saviour.
For he that is mighty hath done to me great things;
    and holy is his name.
And his mercy is on them that fear him from
    generation to generation.
He hath shewed strength with his arm; he hath
    scattered the proud in the imagination of
        their hearts.
He hath put down the mighty from their seats, and
    exalted them of low degree.
He hath filled the hungry with good things; and the
    rich he hath sent empty away.

—LUKE 1:46b–47, 49–53

I am thirsting for your love, my Beloved!
I shall make this body a lamp, and my tender
  heart shall be its wick,
I shall fill it with the scented oil of my young
  love and burn it night and day at Your
  shrine, O Beloved!
For Your love I shall sacrifice all the wealth of
  my youth;
Your name shall be the crown of my head.
I am longing for You, O my Lord: for the season
  of the sowing has come;
      but You are not beside me.

Clouds gather on my brows and my eyes shed
heavy showers.
My parents gave me to You, I have become
Yours for ever; who but You
can be my Lord?
This separation troubles my breast; make me
Your own; make me perfect
like You, O Lord of Perfection!

—MIRABAI

*M*ay the words of my mouth and the meditation of my heart be acceptable to Thee, O Lord, my Strength and my Redeemer.

—JEWISH PRAYER
Conclusion of the "Shemoneh Esrei"

Prayer is in its essence the union of the soul with God. Its effects and fruits are: a pure soul, collection of inner forces, reconciliation with God, tears, forgiveness of sins, a bridge which leads us above and over temptation, a wall of protection against sorrows. It is the work of angels, a food for all spiritual beings, the joy of eternity, a divine action, a source of virtues, a treasury of graces; it is spiritual progress, the food of the soul, revelation, the exclusion of faintheartedness, a prop for our confidence, a comfort in grief.

—St. John Climacus

I asked for strength that I might achieve;
I was made weak that I might learn humbly to
obey.

I asked for health that I might do greater things;
I was given infirmity that I might do better
things.

I asked for riches that I might be happy;
I was given poverty that I might be wise.

I asked for power that I might have the praise of
men;
I was given weakness that I might feel the need
of God.

I asked for all things that I might enjoy life;
I was given life that I might enjoy all things.

I got nothing that I had asked for,
but everything that I had hoped for.
Almost despite myself my unspoken prayers
    were answered;
I am, among all men, most richly blessed.

—PRAYER OF AN UNKNOWN
    CONFEDERATE SOLDIER

$\mathcal{M}$ake us worthy, Lord, to serve our fellow men throughout the world who live and die in poverty and hunger. Give them through our hands this day their daily bread, and by our understanding love, give peace and joy.

—MOTHER TERESA

O Hidden Life vibrant in every
atom;
O Hidden Light! shining in every
creature;
O Hidden Love! embracing all in
Oneness;
May each who feels himself as one
with Thee,
Know he is also one with every
other.

—ANNIE BESANT

*H*oly Spirit,
giving life to all life,
moving all creatures,
root of all things,
washing them clean,
wiping out their mistakes,
healing their wounds,
you are our true life,
luminous, wonderful,
awakening the heart
from its ancient sleep.

—HILDEGARD OF BINGEN

In the beginning was God,
Today is God,
Tomorrow will be God.
Who can make an image of God?
He has no body.
He is the word which comes out of your
    mouth.
That word! It is no more,
It is past, and still it lives!
So is God.

—PYGMY PRAYER

*F*rom all blindness of heart, from pride,
  vainglory, and hypocrisy;
from envy, hatred, and malice, and all
  uncharitableness,
Good Lord, deliver us.

     —THE BOOK OF COMMON PRAYER

$\mathcal{L}$ook to this day,
For it is life,
The very life of life.
In its brief course lie all
The realities and verities of existence,
The bliss of growth,
The splendor of action,
The glory of power—

For yesterday is but a dream,
And tomorrow is only a vision,
But today, well lived,
Makes every yesterday a dream of happiness
And every tomorrow a vision of hope.

—SANSKRIT PROVERB

The world is charged with the grandeur of
   God.
   It will flame out, like shining from
      shook foil;
   It gathers to a greatness, like the ooze of oil
Crushed. Why do men then now not reck
   his rod?
Generations have trod, have trod, have trod;
   And all is seared with trade; bleared,
      smeared with toil;
   And wears man's smudge and shares
      man's smell: the soil
Is bare now, nor can foot feel, being shod.

And for all this, nature is never spent;
   There lives the dearest freshness deep
      down things;
And though the last lights off the black
      West went
   Oh, morning, at the brown brink
      eastward, springs—
Because the Holy Ghost over the bent
   World broods with warm breast and
      with ah! bright wings.

—GERARD MANLEY HOPKINS
"God's Grandeur"

ld I feel discouraged?
Why should the shadows fall?
Why should my heart feel lonely
and long for heaven and home?
When Jesus is my portion
A constant friend is he.

His eye is on the sparrow
And I know he watches me.

I sing because I'm happy,
I sing because I'm free.

His eye is on the sparrow
And I know he watches me.

—AFRICAN-AMERICAN SPIRITUAL

*D*eep peace of the running wave
to you,
Deep peace of the flowing air to you,
Deep peace of the quiet earth to you,
Deep peace of the shining stars to
you,
Deep peace of the Son of Peace to
you.
Amen.

—GAELIC BLESSING

The LORD is my shepherd; I shall not want.
He maketh me to lie down in green pastures:
    he leadeth me beside the still waters.
He restoreth my soul: he leadeth me in the
    paths of righteousness for his name's sake.
Yea, though I walk through the valley of the
    shadow of death, I will fear no evil: for thou
    art with me; thy rod and thy staff they
    comfort me.

Thou prepareset a table before me in the
    presence of mine enemies: thou anointest
    my head with oil; my cup runneth over.
Surely goodness and mercy shall follow me all
    the days of my life: and I will dwell in the
    house of the LORD for ever.

—PSALM 23

*L*et nothing disturb thee,
Nothing affright thee;
All things are passing;
God never changeth;
Patient endurance
Attaineth to all things;
Who God possesseth
In nothing is wanting;
Alone God sufficeth.

—St. Teresa of Avila

Said the Holy One to Israel, "I have told you that when you pray, you should do so in the synagogue in your city. If you cannot pray in the synagogue, pray in your field. If you cannot pray in your field, pray in your house. If you cannot pray in your house, pray on your bed. If you cannot pray on your bed, meditate in your heart."

—MIDRASH PSALMS 4:9

*H*e prayeth best, who loveth
  best
All things both great and small;
For the dear God who loveth us,
He made and loveth all.

—SAMUEL TAYLOR COLERIDGE

O most merciful redeemer, friend,
and brother,
may we know Thee more
    clearly,
love Thee more dearly,
and follow Thee more nearly,
day by day.
Amen.

—RICHARD OF CHICHESTER

e saved . . . and I want to save.

I want to be set free . . . and I want to free.
  Amen.
I want to be born . . . and I want to give birth.
  Amen.
I want to hear . . . and I want to be heard.
Sweetness dances. I want to pipe; all of you
  dance. Amen.
I want to run away . . . and I want to stay.
  Amen.
I want to make you beautiful . . . and I want to
  be beautiful. Amen.

I want to join with you . . . and I want to be
   joined. Amen.

I have no house . . . and I have houses. Amen.
I have no ground . . . and I have ground. Amen.
I have no temple . . . and I have temples. Amen.
If you look at me . . . I will be a lamp. Amen.
If you see me . . . I will be a mirror. Amen.
If you knock on me . . . I will be a door. Amen.
If you are a traveler . . . I will be a road. Amen.

This is my dance . . . Answer me with dancing.

—THE ACTS OF JOHN

Chilly water, chilly water,
Hallelujah to that lamb.
I know that water is chilly and cold,
Hallelujah to that lamb.
But I have Jesus in my soul,
Hallelujah to that lamb.
Satan's just like a snake in the grass
Hallelujah to that lamb.
He's watching for to bite you as you pass
Hallelujah to that lamb.

—AFRICAN-AMERICAN SPIRITUAL

$\mathcal{C}$hrist has no body now on earth but yours;
yours are the only hands with which he can do
   his work,
yours are the only feet with which he can go
   about the world,
yours are the only eyes through which his
   compassion can shine forth upon a troubled
      world.
Christ has no body on earth now but yours.

—ST. TERESA OF AVILA

$\mathcal{L}$ove bade me welcome: yet my soul drew
  back,
  Guiltie of dust and sinne.
But quick-ey'd Love, observing me grow slack
  From my first entrance in,
Drew nearer to me, sweetly questioning
  If I lack'd any thing.

"A guest," I answer'd, "worthy to be here":
  Love said, "You shall be he."
"I the unkinde, ungratefull? Ah, my deare,
  I cannot look on thee."
Love took my hand, and smiling did reply,
  "Who made the eyes but I?"

"Truth Lord, but I have marr'd them: let my
  shame
  Go where it doth deserve."
"And know you not," sayes Love, "who bore
  the blame?"
  "My deare, then I will serve."
"You must sit down," sayes Love, "and taste
  my meat":
  So I did sit and eat.

—GEORGE HERBERT
"A Dialogue Between God and the Soul"

$\mathcal{L}$ooking down into my father's
dead face
for the last time
my mother said without
tears, without smiles
without regrets
but with *civility*
"Goodnight, Willie Lee, I'll see you
in the morning."
And it was then I knew that the healing
of all our wounds
is forgiveness
That permits a promise of our return
at the end.

—ALICE WALKER

*M*ay all beings have happiness, and the
   causes of happiness;
May all be free from sorrow, and the causes of
   sorrow;
May all never be separated from the sacred
   happiness which is sorrowless;
And may all live in equanimity, without too
   much attachment and too much aversion,
And live believing in the equality of all that
   lives.

—BUDDHIST PRAYER

*M*ake me pure, Lord:
Thou art holy:
Make me meek, Lord:
Thou wert lowly.

—GERARD MANLEY HOPKINS

*M*ore things are wrought
by prayer than this world
dreams of.

—ALFRED, LORD TENNYSON

Blessed are the poor in spirit:
   for their's is the kingdom of heaven.
Blessed are they that mourn:
   for they shall be comforted.
Blessed are the meek:
   for they shall inherit the earth.
Blessed are they which do hunger
   and thirst after righteousness:
      for they shall be filled.

Blessed are the merciful:
   for they shall obtain mercy.
Blessed are the pure in heart:
   for they shall see God.
Blessed are the peacemakers:
   for they shall be called the children of God.
Blessed are they which are persecuted
   for righteousness' sake:
      for their's is the kingdom of heaven.

—MATTHEW 5:3–10

*S*ir spirit, forgive me my sins,
Sir spirit give me your blessing
  again,
Sir Spirit forgive my phantom
  body's demands,
Sir Spirit thanks for your kindness
  past. . . .

—ALLEN GINSBERG
"Elegy for Neal Cassady"

*B*ecause between now and
tomorrow, maybe I, God, will
have passed by your way . . .
Blessed is he who puts off, that is
to say,
Blessed is he who hopes. And who
sleeps.

—CHARLES PÉGUY

*M*ay the power of God this day enable me,
the nakedness of God disarm me,
the beauty of God silence me,
the justice of God give me voice,
the integrity of God hold me,
the desire of God move me,
the fear of God expose me to the truth,
the breath of God give me abundant life.

—JANET MORLEY

$\mathcal{L}$et our sleeping soul
remember, and be awake and
be alive, in contemplation, of
how our life passes away, of
how our death comes
forward to us, so silently.

—JORGE MANRIQUE

*L*iving beings are without
number: I vow to row them to
the other shore.
Defilements are without number: I
vow to remove them from myself.
The teachings are immeasurable: I
vow to study and practice them.
The way is very long: I vow to
arrive at the end.

—FOUR VOWS OF THE BODDHISATTVA

Meditation, then, is bringing the mind home.

—SOGYAL RINPOCHE

*W*e were enclosed,
O eternal Father,
within the garden of your breast.
You drew us out of your holy mind
like a flower
petaled with our soul's three
  powers,
and into each power
you put the whole plant,
so that they might bear fruit in
  your garden,

might come back to you
with the fruit you gave them.
And you would come back to the
   soul,
to fill her with your blessedness.
There the soul dwells—
like the fish in the sea
and the sea in the fish.

—St. Catherine of Siena

As the bridegroom rejoiceth over the bride, so shall thy God rejoice over thee.

—ISAIAH 62:5

*M*ay the road rise up to meet you.
May the wind be always at your back.
May the sun shine warm upon your face,
the rains fall soft upon your fields
and until we meet again,
may God hold you in the palm of His hand.

—GAELIC BLESSING

Cut through, O lord,
my heart's greed,
and show me
your way out.

O lord white as jasmine.

———◆———

After this body has known my lord
    who cares if it feeds
    a dog
    or soaks up water?

Like an elephant
lost from his herd
suddenly captured,

remembering his mountains,
    his Vindhyas,
    I remember.

O lord white as jasmine
show me
your ways.
    Call me: Child, come here,
    come this way.

—MAHADEVIYAKKA

King of Glorie, King of Peace,
  I will love thee;
And that love may never cease,
  I will move thee.

Thou hast granted my request,
  Thou hast heard me;
Thou didst note my working breast,
  Thou hast spar'd me.

Wherefore with my utmost art
   I will sing thee,
And the cream of all my heart
   I will bring thee.

———◆———

Small it is, in this poor sort
   To enrol thee:
E'en eternitie's too short
   To extol thee.

—GEORGE HERBERT

Thou my mother, and my father
  thou
Thou my friend, and my teacher
  thou
Thou my wisdom, and my riches
  thou
Thou art all to me, O God of all
  Gods.

—RAMANUJA INDIAN PRAYER

Better than a hundred years lived in ignorance,
   without contemplation, is one single day of life
   lived in wisdom and in deep contemplation.
Better than a hundred years lived in idleness and in
   weakness is a single day of life lived with courage
   and powerful striving.
Better than a hundred years not considering how all
   things arise and pass away is one single day of life
   if one considers how all things arise and pass
   away.
Better than a hundred years not seeing one's own
   immortality is one single day of life if one sees
   one's own immortality.

—THE DHAMMAPADA

*N*ight is drawing nigh.
For all that has been—
   Thanks!
For all that shall be—
   Yes!

—DAG HAMMARSKJÖLD

*I*t is prayer that restores to us the ability to feel, to see, and to appreciate.

—Reuven Hammer

Rejoice evermore. Pray without ceasing. In every thing give thanks.

—1 Thessalonians 5:16–18

i thank You God for most this
    amazing
day:for the leaping greenly spirits of
    trees
and a blue true dream of sky;and
    for everything
which is natural which is infinite
    which is yes

—E.E. CUMMINGS

*W*e thankfully acknowledge You,
   O Lord our God,
for granting our ancestors the inheritance of a
   pleasant, good, and spacious land,
for taking us out of the land of Egypt, O Lord
   our God, and redeeming us from the house
   of bondage,
for the covenant which You have implanted in
   our flesh,
for the Torah which You have taught us,
for the laws which You have revealed to us,
for life, grace, and kindness which You have
   bestowed upon us,

and for the food with which You always provide
   us, every day, at all seasons and times.
For all this do we thankfully acknowledge You
   and bless You
—may Your name be continually blessed by all
   living beings forever and ever—
as it is written: When you have eaten your fill,
   bless the Lord your God for the good land
   which He has given you (Dt. 8:10).

—JEWISH MEALTIME BLESSING
"Birkat Ha-Mazon"

Omy God,
the soul You have placed within me is pure.
You created it, You formed it, You breathed it
within me, You guard it within me, You will
take it from me in the future and will restore it
to me in the future-to-come.
As long as the soul is within me I thankfully
acknowledge You, O Lord my God and God of
my fathers, Master of all deeds, Lord of all souls.
Blessed are You, O Lord, who restores souls to
the dead.

—THE TALMUD

*O*God, give me, I pray Thee,
light on my right hand
and light on my left hand
and light above me
and light beneath me,
O Lord, increase light within me
and give me light
and illuminate me.

—ASCRIBED TO MUHAMMAD

$\mathcal{L}$ike a golden beacon signaling
   on a moonless night,
Tao guides our passage through this
   transitory realm.
In moments of darkness and pain
remember all is cyclical.
Sit quietly behind; your wooden
   door:
Spring will come again.

—LOY CHING YUEN

I will extol thee, O LORD; for thou hast lifted me
   up, and hast not made my foes to rejoice over me.
O LORD my God, I cried unto thee, and thou hast
   healed me.
O LORD, thou hast brought up my soul from the
   grave: thou hast kept me alive, that I should not
   go down to the pit.
Sing unto the LORD, O ye saints of his, and give
   thanks at the remembrance of his holiness.
For his anger endureth but a moment; in his favour is
   life: weeping may endure for a night, but joy
   cometh in the morning.

—PSALM 30:1–5

*E*arth our mother, breathe forth life
　all night sleeping
　　now awaking
　in the east
　now see the dawn

Earth our mother, breathe and waken
　leaves are stirring
　all things moving
　new day coming
life renewing

—PAWNEE PRAYER

*B*less
something small
but infinite
and quiet.

There are senses
make an object
in their simple
feeling for one.

—ROBERT CREELEY
"A Prayer"

*W*e return thanks to our mother,
   the earth, which sustains us.
We return thanks to the rivers and streams,
   which supply us with water.
We return thanks to all herbs,
   which furnish medicines for the cure to our
   diseases.
We return thanks to the corn, and to her sisters,
   the beans and squashes,
   which give us life.
We return thanks to the bushes and trees,
   which provide us with fruit.
We return thanks to the wind,
   which, moving in the air, has banished diseases.

We return thanks to the moon and stars,
   which have given to us their light
   when the sun was gone.
We return thanks to our grandfather Hé-no,
   that he has protected his grandchildren
   from witches and reptiles,
   and has given to us his rain.
We return thanks to the sun,
   that he has looked upon the earth
   with a beneficent eye.
Lastly, we return thanks to the Great Spirit,
   in whom is embodied all goodness,
   and who directs all things
   for the good of his children.

—IROQUOIS PRAYER

If He had fed us with manna,
and had not given us the Sabbath,
it would have sufficed.

If He had given us the Sabbath,
and had not brought us to
Mount Sinai,
it would have sufficed.

If He had brought us near to
Mount Sinai,
and had not given us the Law,
it would have sufficed.

If He had given us the Law,
and had not led us into the land
of Israel,
it would have sufficed.

If He had led us into the land
of Israel
and not built the temple,
it would have sufficed.

—JEWISH PRAYER FOR PASSOVER
"Dayanu"

*L*ord, I am grateful to You
that in Your mysterious love
You have taken away from me
all earthly wealth,
and that You now clothe and feed me
through the kindness of others.

Lord, I am grateful to You
that since You have taken away from me
the sight of my eyes.
You care for me now
through the eyes of others.

Lord, I am grateful to You
that since you have taken away from me
the strength of my hands and heart,
you care for me now
through the hands and hearts of others.

Lord, I pray for them,
that You will reward them in Your love,
that they may continue to faithfully serve and
care until they come to a happy end
in eternity with You.

—MECHTHILD OF MAGDEBURG

This ritual is one.
The food is one.
We who offer the food are one.
The fire of hunger is also one.
All action is one.
We who understand this are one.

—ANCIENT HINDU BLESSING

Prayer is for the soul, what food is for the body. The blessing of one prayer lasts until the next, just as the strength gained from one meal lasts till the one after.

—JEWISH PRAYER

Blessed are you,
O Lord Our God,
Eternal King,

Who feeds the whole world
With your goodness,—
With grace, with loving kindness,
And with tender mercy.

You give food to all flesh,
For Your loving kindness endures forever.
Through Your great goodness,
Food has never failed us.
O may it not fail us forever;

For Your name's sake, since You
Nourish and sustain all living things
And do good to all,
And provide food for all Your creatures
Whom You have created.

Blessed are You, O Lord,
Who gives food to all.

—ANCIENT JEWISH BLESSING

Be with me, O God, at
  breaking of bread,
Be with me, O God, at the close of
  my meal;
Let no whit adown my body
That may hurt my sorrowing soul.
O no whit adown my body
That may hurt my sorrowing soul.

—GAELIC GRACE

The bread is pure and
   fresh,
the water is cool and clear.
Lord of all life, be with us,
Lord of all life, be near.

—AFRICAN GRACE

O my brothers of the wilderness,
My little brothers,
For my necessities
I am about to kill you!
May the Master of Life who made you
In the form of the quarry
That the children may be fed,
Speedily provide you
Another house;
So there may be peace
Between me and thy spirit.

—MARY AUSTIN

$\mathcal{L}$ord, behold our family here assembled.
We thank you for this place in which we dwell,
for the love that unites us,
for the peace accorded us this day,
for the hope with which we expect the morrow;
for the health, the work, the food and the bright
    skies
that make our lives delightful;
for our friends in all parts of the earth. Amen.

— ROBERT LOUIS STEVENSON

*O*ur father, hear us, and our
  grandfather. I mention also
  all those that shine, the
  yellow day, the good wind,
  the good timber, and the good earth.
All the animals, listen to me
  under the ground. Animals
  above ground, and water
  animals, listen to me. We
  shall eat your remnants of
  food. Let them be good.
Let there be long breath and life.
  Let the people increase, the

children of all ages, the girls
and the boys, and the men
of all ages and the women,
the old men of all ages and
the old women. The food
will give us strength
whenever
the sun runs.
Listen to us, Father, Grandfather.
We ask thought, heart,
love, happiness. We are
going to eat.

—ARAPAHO PRAYER BEFORE EATING

The food which we are about to eat
Is Earth, Water and Sun, compounded through
the alchemy of many plants.
Therefore Earth, Water and Sun will become
part of us.
This food is also the fruit of the labor of many
beings and creatures.
We are grateful for it.

May it give us strength, health, joy.

And may it increase our love.

—Unitarian Prayer

We venerate the Three
   Treasures:
Buddha, Dharma, Sangha,
And are thankful for this meal,
The work of many people
And the sharing of other forms of
   life.

—ZEN PRAYER

First, seventy-two labors brought us this
   food,
We should know how it comes to us.
Second, as we receive this offering,
We should consider
Whether our virtue and practice deserve it.
Third, as we desire the natural order of mind,
To be free from clinging,
We must be free from greed.
Fourth, to support our life, we take this food.
Fifth, to attain our way we take this food.
First, this food is for the Three Treasures.
Second, it is for our teachers, parents, nation,

And all sentient beings.
Third, it is for all beings in the three worlds.
Thus, we eat this food with everyone,
We eat to stop all evil, to practice good,
To save all sentient beings,
And to accomplish our Buddha Way.

—MEAL GATHA

*L*et us not forget what Thou hast done for us, and when Thy helping hand hath wondrously been there, then let us not seek it again as ungrateful beings who only ate and were satisfied.

—SØREN KIERKEGAARD

*A*nd when thou prayest, thou shalt not be as the hypocrites are: for they love to pray standing in the synagogues and in the corners of the streets, that they may be seen of men. Verily I say unto you, They have their reward.

But thou, when thou prayest, enter into thy closet, and when thou hast shut thy door, pray to thy Father which is in secret; and thy Father which seeth in secret shall reward thee openly.

—MATTHEW 6:5–6

That you may have pleasure in
  everything
Seek your own pleasure in nothing.
That you may know everything
Seek to know nothing.
That you may possess all things
Seek to possess nothing.
That you may be everything
Seek to be nothing.

—St. John of the Cross

'Tis the gift to be simple,
'Tis the gift to be free,
'Tis the gift to come down
Where we ought to be—
And when we find ourselves
In the place just right,
'Twill be in the valley
Of love and delight.
When true simplicity is gained,
To bow and to bend
We shan't be asham'd,
To turn, turn will be our delight,
Till by turning, turning
We come round right.

—SHAKER HYMN

OM.

This eternal Word is all: what
was, what is and what shall
be, and what beyond is in
eternity. All is

OM.

—THE UPANISHADS

The fewer the words,
the better the prayer.

—Martin Luther

*M*ay there be peace in the higher regions;
may there be peace in the firmament; may
there be peace on earth. May the waters flow
peacefully; may the herbs and plants grow
peacefully; may all the divine powers bring
unto us peace. The supreme Lord is peace. May
we all be in peace, peace, and only peace; and
may that peace come unto each of us.

Shanti—Shanti—Shanti!
(Peace—Peace—Peace!)

—THE VEDAS

Come, my beloved, let us greet the bride, let us welcome Shabbos, A peaceful and blessed Shabbos.

—SABBATH PRAYER

O God, you have formed
heaven and earth;
You have given me all the
  goods
that the earth bears!
Here is your part, my God.
Take it!

—PRAYER FROM ZAIRE

*G*rant me to recogni
other men, Lord God, the
radiance of your own face.

—TEILHARD DE CHARDIN

*I*f I spent enough time
with the tiniest creature—
even a caterpillar—
I would never have to
prepare a sermon. So full of
God is every creature.

—MEISTER ECKHART

*H*ere I am at Your service,
  O Lord, here I am.
Here I am. No partner do You have.
  Here I am.
Truly, the praise and the favor is
  Yours, and the dominion.
No partner do You have.

—MUSLIM PRAYER
"Talbiyyah"

*L*ate have I loved you, O beauty
so ancient and so new;
   late have I loved you.
You called and cried to me and
broke upon my deafness;
   and you sent forth your light
and shone upon me,
and chased away my blindness;

You breathed fragrance upon me,
   and I drew in my breath and do
not pant for you:
I tasted you and I now hunger and
thirst for you;
   you touched me, and I have
burned for your peace.

—St. Augustine

I pray Thee, O gracious Lord,
Grant that this mendicant may cling
   successfully to solitude,
Making solitude his paradise.

—BUDDHIST PRAYER

*F*or prayer is a request. The essence of request, as distinct from compulsion, is that it may or may not be granted.

—C.S. LEWIS

I want to want to want to want you God.

—MICHAEL RAMSEY

You, whose day it is, make it beautiful. Get out your rainbow colors, so it will be beautiful.

—NOOTKA SONG

Lord, make me an instrument of your
    peace.
Where there is hatred, let me sow
    love,
Where there is injury, pardon;
Where there is doubt, faith;
Where there is despair, hope;
Where there is darkness, light;
And where there is sadness, joy.

O, Divine Master, grant that I may not
    so much
    seek to be consoled as to console,
    to be understood as to understand,
    to be loved, as to love.

For it is in giving that we receive,
    it is in pardoning that we are
        pardoned,
    and it is in dying that we are born to
        eternal life.

—St. Francis of Assisi

*S*pirit of the living God,
 fall afresh on us.
Spirit of the living God,
  fall afresh on us.
Melt us, mould us,
 fill us, use us.
Spirit of the living God,
  fall afresh on us.

—MICHAEL IVERSON

O Thou who art at home
Deep in my heart
Enable me to join you
Deep in my heart.

—THE TALMUD

*N*ow this day,
My sun father,
Now that you have come out
standing to your sacred place,
That from which we draw the
water of life,
Prayer meal
Here I give you.

Your long life,
Your old age,
Your waters,
Your seeds,
Your riches,
Your power,
Your strong spirit,
All these to me may you grant.

—ZUÑI PRAYER AT SUNRISE

Oh Allah! I ask Thee for joyful patience, great reward; sincere turning; a remembering tongue; forbearing body; increased subsistence, beneficial knowledge and good action; granted supplication; forgiven sin; honest livelihood; decent children; wholesome cure; a blessed destination; a victory close at hand; and lasting bliss and the Paradise, and silk, and freshness and vigour, and delight, by Thy mercy, Oh Most Merciful of the Merciful!

—MUSLIM PRAYER
"Namaz-e-Isha"

I cannot dance, O Lord,
Unless You lead me.
If You wish me to leap joyfully,
Let me see You dance and sing—

Then I will leap into Love—
And from Love into Knowledge,
And from Knowledge into the Harvest,
That sweetest Fruit beyond human sense.

There I will stay with You, whirling.

—MECHTHILD OF MAGDEBURG

Come, Holy Spirit,
And send out from heaven
The beam of your light.

—ARCHBISHOP STEPHEN LANGTON
"The Golden Sequence," Whitsunday

Sun, my relative
Be good coming out
Do something good for us.

Make me work,
So I can do anything in the garden
I hoe, I plant corn, I irrigate.

You, sun, be good going down at sunset
We lay down to sleep I want to feel good.

While I sleep you come up.
Go on your course many times.
Make good things for us men.

Make me always the same as I am now.

—HAVASUPAI PRAYER

*H*ere's the thing, say Shug. The thing I believe. God is inside you and inside everybody else. You come into the world with God. But only them that search for it inside find it. And sometimes it just manifest itself even if you not looking, or don't know what you looking for. Trouble do it for most folks, I think. Sorrow, lord. Feeling like shit.

It? I ast.

Yeah, It. God ain't a he or a she, but a It.

But what do it look like? I ast.

Don't look like nothing, she say. It ain't a picture show. It ain't something you can look at apart from anything else, including yourself. I believe God is everything, say Shug. Everything that is or ever was or ever will be. And when you can feel that, and be happy to feel that, you've found It.

Shug a beautiful something, let me tell you. She frown a little, look out cross the yard, lean back in her chair, look like a big rose.

She say, My first step from the old white man was trees. Then air. Then birds. Then other people. But one day when I was sitting quiet and feeling like a motherless child, which I was, it come to me: that feeling of being part of everything, not separate at all. I knew that if I cut a tree, my arm would bleed. And I laughed and I cried and I run all round the house. I knew just what it was. In fact, when it happen, you can't miss it.

—ALICE WALKER
The Color Purple

O our Father the Sky, hear us
  and make us bold.
O our Mother the Earth, hear us
  and give us support.
O Spirit of the East,
  send us your Wisdom.
O Spirit of the South,
  may we walk your path of life.
O Spirit of the West,
  may we always be ready for the long journey.
O Spirit of the North, purify us
  with your cleansing winds.

—SIOUX PRAYER

Say your prayers in a melody that is most pleasant and sweet to you. Then you shall pray with proper *kavanah*, because the melody will draw your heart after the words come from your mouth. Supplicate in a melody that makes the heart weep, praise in a melody that makes the heart glad.

—RABBI HAYIM HALEVY DONIN

*L*ord of the springtime, Father of flower, field and fruit, smile on us in these earnest days when the work is heavy and the toil wearisome; lift up our hearts, O God, to the things worthwhile—sunshine and night, the dripping rain, the song of the birds, books and music, and the voices of our friends. Lift up our hearts to these this night and grant us Thy peace. Amen.

—W.E.B. Du Bois

*C*ome, true light.

Come, life eternal.

Come, hidden mystery.

Come, treasure without name.

Come, rejoicing without end

Come, light that knows no evening.

Come, raising of the fallen.

Come, resurrection of the dead.

Come, for you are yourself the desire that is
    within me.

Come, my breath and my life.

Come, the consolation of my humble soul.

Come, my joy, my glory, my endless delight.

—St. Symeon

*E*arth teach me stillness
  as the grasses are stilled with light.
Earth teach me suffering
  as old stones suffer with memory.
Earth teach me humility
  as blossoms are humble with beginning.
Earth teach me caring
  as the mother who secures her young.
Earth teach me courage
  as the tree which stands all alone.
Earth teach me limitation
  as the ant which crawls on the ground.

Earth teach me freedom
    as the eagle which soars in the sky.
Earth teach me resignation
    as the leaves which die in the fall.
Earth teach me regeneration
    as the seed which rises in the spring.
Earth teach me to forget myself
    as melted snow forgets its life.
Earth teach me to remember kindness
    as dry fields weep with rain.

—UTE PRAYER

*L*ord, I have loved Your sky,
Be it said against or for me,
Have loved it clear and high,
Or low and stormy;

Till I have reeled and stumbled
From looking up too much,
And fallen and been humbled
To wear a crutch.

My love for every Heaven
O'er which You, Lord, have lorded,
From number One to Seven,
Should be rewarded.

It may not give me hope
That when I am translated
My scalp will in the cope
Be constellated.

But if that seems to tend
To my undue renown,
At least it ought to send
Me up, not down.

—ROBERT FROST
"Astrometaphysical"

O heavenly Father, protect and bless all things that have breath: guard them from all evil and let them sleep in peace.

—ALBERT SCHWEITZER
"A Child's Prayer"

That our earth mother may wrap herself
In a fourfold robe of white meal;
That she may be covered with frost flowers;
That yonder on all the mossy mountains
The forests may huddle together with the cold;
That their arms may be broken by the snow,
in order that the land may be thus,
I have made my prayer sticks into living beings.

—ZUÑI OFFERING

The LORD bless thee, and keep thee: The LORD make his face shine upon thee, and be gracious unto thee: The LORD lift up his countenance upon thee, and give thee peace.

—NUMBERS 6:24–26

*C*ome, Holy Spirit, fill the hearts
of your faithful,
and enkindle in them the fire of
your love.
Send forth your Spirit and they
shall be created.
And you shall renew the face of the
earth.
Let us pray.

—ATTRIBUTED TO RABANUS MAURUS

*O*great God of Heaven,
Draw Thou my soul to Thyself
That I may make repentance
With a right and a strong heart,
With a heart broken and contrite,
That shall not change nor bend nor yield.

O great God of the angels,
Bring Thou me to the dwelling of peace;
O great God of the angels,
Preserve me from the evil of the fairies;
O great God of the angels,
Bathe me in the bathing of Thy pool.

—CELTIC PRAYER

Father in Heaven! Reawaken conscience in our breast. Make us bend the ear of the spirit to Thy voice, so that we may perceive Thy will for us in its clear purity as it is in Heaven, pure of our false worldly wisdom, unstifled by the voice of passion; keep us vigilant so that we may work for our salvation with fear and trembling; oh, but grant also that when the Law speaks most strongly, when its seriousness fills us with dread, when the thunder booms from Sinai—Oh grant that we may hear also a gentle voice murmuring to us that we are Thy children, so that we will cry with joy, Abba, Father.

—SØREN KIERKEGAARD

*J*esus, will you come by here
O Jesus, will you come by here
Jesus will you come by here.
Now is a needed time
O now is a needed time
Now is a needed time.

Come if you don't stay long
O come if you don't stay long
Come if you don't stay long.
Now is a needed time
O now is a needed time
Now is a needed time.

Prayin' for you to come by here
I'm prayin' for you to come by here
Jesus won't you come by here, come by here.
Now is a needed time
Right now Lord is a needed time
Now is a needed time.

———◆———

Down on my knees an' prayin'
Down on my knees an' prayin'
Jesus won't you come by here.
Jesus won't you come by here
O Jesus won't you come by here
Jesus won't you come by here.

—LIGHTNIN' HOPKINS
"NEEDED TIME"

*M*ay Heaven guard and keep you,
Cause your grain to prosper,
Send you nothing that is not good.
May you receive from Heaven a
    hundred boons,
May Heaven send down to you
    blessings so many
That the day is not long enough for
    them all.

—THE BOOK OF SONGS
"Blessings on Gentle Folk"

*I*n prayer,
come empty,
do nothing.

—ST. JOHN OF THE CROSS

Take time to listen to what is said without words, to obey the law too subtle to be written, to worship the unnameable and to embrace the unformed.

—LAO-TZU

Friend, if thou wilt be
   something, stand not still:
Thou must from one light to
   another go.

—ANGELUS SILESIUS

*H*o! Sun, Moon, Stars, all that move in
the heavens
I bid you hear me!
Into your midst has come a new life.
Consent, I implore you!
Make its path smooth, that it may reach
the brow of the first hill!

Ho! You Winds, Clouds, Rain, Mist,
all you that move in the air,
I bid you hear me!
Into your midst has come a new life.
Consent, I implore you!
Make its path smooth, that it may reach
the brow of the second hill!

Ho! You Hills, Valleys, Rivers, Lakes,
    Trees, Grasses, all you of the earth.
I bid you hear me!
Into your midst has come a new life.
Consent, I implore you.
    Make its path smooth, that it may reach
    the brow of the third hill!

—OMAHA PRAYER

*G*ive us, Lord, a humble, quiet, peaceable, patient, tender and charitable mind, and in all our thoughts, words and deeds a taste of the Holy Spirit. Give us, Lord, a lively faith, a firm hope, a fervent charity, a love of you. Take from us all lukewarmness in meditation, dullness in prayer. Give us fervour and delight in thinking of you and your grace, your tender compassion towards me. The things that we pray for, good Lord, give us grace to labour for: through Jesus Christ our Lord.

—St. Thomas More

The best help in all action is—to pray, that is true genius; then one never goes wrong.

—Søren Kierkegaard

*L*et me seek you in my desire,
Let me desire you in my seeking.
Let me find you by loving you
Let me love you when I find you.

—St. Anselm

*O*our Mother the Earth, O our Father the Sky,
Your children are we, and with tired backs
We bring you the gifts you love.
Then weave for us a garment of brightness;
May the warp be the white light of morning,
May the weft be the red light of evening,
May the fringes be the falling rain,
May the border be the standing rainbow.
Thus weave for us a garment of brightness,
That we may walk fittingly where birds sing,
That we may walk fittingly where grass is green,
O our Mother the Earth, O our Father the Sky.

—TEWA PRAYER
"Song of the Sky Loom"

O Heavenly King, the Comforter, the Spirit of Truth who art everywhere and fillest all things. Treasury of Blessings, and Giver of Life: Come and abide in us, and cleanse us from every impurity, and save our souls, O Good One.

O most-holy Trinity: have mercy on us. O Lord: cleanse us from our sins. O Master: pardon our transgressions. O Holy One: visit and heal our infirmities, for Thy name's sake.

—ST. JOHN CHRYSOSTOM

*F*orgive, O Lord, my little jokes
   on Thee
And I'll forgive Thy great big one
   on me.

—ROBERT FROST
In the Clearing

*M*y period had come for Prayer—
No other Art—would do—
My Tactics missed a rudiment—
Creator—Was it you?

God grows above—so those who pray
Horizons—must ascend—
And so I stepped upon the North
To see this Curious Friend—

His House was not—no sign had He—
By Chimney—nor by Door
Could I infer his Residence—
Vast Prairies of Air

Unbroken by a Settler—
Were all that I could see—
Infinitude—Had'st Thou no Face
That I might look on Thee?

The Silence condescended—
Creation stopped—for Me—
But awed beyond my errand—
I worshipped—did not "pray"—

—EMILY DICKINSON

*J*esus, lover of my soul,
Let me to Thy bosom fly,
While the waters nearer roll,
While the tempest still is high;
Hide me, O my Savior, hide,
Till the storm of life is past;
Safe into the haven glide,
O receive my soul at last.

—CHARLES WESLEY
"Jesus, Lover of My Soul"

$\mathcal{L}$ord Jesus Christ, pierce my sou
love so that I may always long for y
who are the bread of angels and the ......nent
of the soul's deepest desires. . . . May my soul
thirst for you, who are the source of life,
wisdom, knowledge, light and all the riches of
God our Father. May I always seek and find
you, think upon you, speak to you and do all
things for the honour and glory of your holy
name. Be always my only hope, my peace, my
refuge and my help in whom my heart is rooted
so that I may never be separated from you.

—St. Bonaventure

O Lord, grant me to greet the coming day in peace. Help me in all things to rely upon thy holy will. In every hour of the day reveal thy will to me. Bless my dealings with all who surround me. Teach me to treat all that comes to me throughout the day with peace of soul, and with firm conviction that thy will governs all. In all my deeds and words guide my thoughts and feelings. In unforeseen events let me not forget that all are sent by thee. Teach me to act firmly and wisely, without embittering and embarrassing others. Give me strength to bear the fatigue of the coming day with all that it shall bring. Direct my will, teach me to pray, pray thou thyself in me. Amen.

—EASTERN ORTHODOX PRAYER

O abyss, O Eternal Godhead, O sea profound, what more could you give me than yourself? You are the fire that ever burns without being consumed; you consume in your heat all the soul's self-love; you are the fire which takes away cold; with your light you illuminate me so that I may know all your truth. Clothe me, clothe me with yourself, Eternal Truth, so that I may run this mortal life with true obedience, and with the light of your most holy faith.

—St. Catherine of Siena

Beloved Lord, Almighty God!
Through the rays of the sun,
Through the waves of the air,
Through the All-pervading Life in
   space,
Purify and revivify me, and, I pray.
Heal my body, heart, and soul.
                    Amen.

—HAZRAT INAYAT KHAN

You made me to find you; give me strength to seek you. My strength and my weakness are in your hands: preserve my strength and help my weakness. Where you have opened the door, let me enter in; where it is shut, open to my knocking.

Let me ever increase in remembering you, understanding you, loving you, until you restore me to your perfect pattern.

—ST. AUGUSTINE

*G*ive us a pure heart that we may
    see thee,
A humble heart that we may hear
    thee,
A heart of love that we may serve
    thee,
A heart of faith that we may love
    thee.

—DAG HAMMARSKJÖLD

I love you Jesus, my love, above
all things;
I repent with my whole heart for
having offended you.
Never permit me to separate myself
from you again.
Grant that I may love you always
then do with me what you will.

—THE STATIONS OF THE CROSS

*F*rom the blossoming lotus of devotion, at t
  center of my heart,
Rise up, O compassionate master, my only
  refuge!
I am plagued by past actions and turbulent
  emotions:
To protect me in my misfortune
Remain as the jewel-ornament on the crown of
  my head, the mandala of great bliss,
Arousing all my mindfulness and awareness, I
  pray!

—JIKMÉ LINGRA

243

...ts on my pillow
...your mercy.

...on my mattress,
Let my soul relax in your peace.

As my body finds warmth beneath the
    blankets,
Let my soul find warmth in your love.

As my mind is filled with dreams,
Let my soul be filled with visions of heaven.

—JOHANN FREYLINGHAUSEN

*A*nd the best prayer . . . bursts freely forth from the heart to God, when urgency and need put the words into the mouth. Yea, a prayer acceptable unto God can be uttered without words, through the fervent silent cry of the soul, in sighs, longings and groanings of the heart. . . .

—EPHRAIM PRETORIUS

*I*nto thine hand I commit
　　my spirit:
thou hast redeemed me,
　　O LORD God of truth.

—PSALM 31:5

$\mathcal{L}$et the lost millions pray it in the dark!
My failure is no different from Jonah's.
We both have lacked the courage in the heart
To overcome the fear within the soul
And go ahead to any accomplishment.
Courage is what it takes and takes the more of
Because the deeper fear is so eternal.
And if I say we lift him from the floor
And lay him where you ordered him to lie
Before the cross, it is from fellow-feeling,
As if I asked for one more chance myself
To learn to say
Nothing can make injustice just but mercy.

—Robert Frost
A Masque of Mercy

I will lift up mine eyes unto the hills, from
   whence cometh my help.

My help cometh from the LORD, which made
   heaven and earth.

He will not suffer thy foot to be moved: he that
   keepeth thee will not slumber.

Behold, he that keepeth Israel shall neither
   slumber nor sleep.

The LORD is thy keeper: the LORD is thy shade
   upon thy right hand.

The sun shall not smite thee by day, nor the
   moon by night.
The LORD shall preserve thee from all evil: he
   shall preserve thy soul.
The LORD shall preserve thy going out and thy
   coming in from this time forth, and even for
   evermore.

—PSALM 121

Take, O Lord, and receive
all my liberty,
my memory,
my understanding,
and my entire will,
all that I have and possess.
You have given all to me.
To you, O Lord, I return it.
All is Yours, dispose of it
wholly according to Your will.
Give me Your love and Your grace,
for this is sufficient for me.

—St. Ignatius Loyola

O living flame of love
That wounds so tenderly
In my soul's deepest centre.
As you are no longer oppressive
Perfect your work in me if it is
    your will.
Break the web of this sweet
    encounter.

—ST. JOHN OF THE CROSS

O Merciful God, who answerest
the poor,
      Answer us,
O Merciful God, who answerest the
lowly in spirit,
      Answer us,
O Merciful God, who answerest the
broken of heart,
      Answer us.
O Merciful God,
      Answer us.

O Merciful God,
> Have compassion.

O Merciful God,
> Redeem.

O Merciful God,
> Save.

O Merciful God, have pity upon us,
> Now,
> Speedily,
> And at a near time.

—JEWISH PRAYER FOR THE
DAY OF ATONEMENT

At God's door—how could I
   knock now,
For I have no hand or heart now?
You have carried heart and hand,
   God!
Grant me safety, God forgive
   me. . . .

—JALALUDDIN RUMI
"Evening Prayer"

*B*ut give me the strength that waits upon You in silence and peace. Give me humility in which alone is rest, and deliver me from pride which is the heaviest of burdens.

—THOMAS MERTON

Precious Lord, take my hand.
Lead me on. Let me stand.
I am tired. I am weak. I am worn.
Through the storm,
Through the night,
Lead me on to the light.
Take my hand, precious Lord,
and lead me home

—AFRICAN-AMERICAN SPIRITUAL

Protect me, O Lord;
My boat is so small,
And your sea is so big.

—BRETON FISHERMAN'S PRAYER

O God, early in the morning I cry to you.
Help me to pray
And to concentrate my thoughts on you:
I cannot do this alone.

In me there is darkness,
But with you there is light;
I am lonely, but you do not leave me;
I am feeble in heart, but with you there is help;
I am restless, but with you there is peace.
In me there is bitterness, but with you there is
    patience;
I do not understand your ways,
But you know the way for me . . .

Restore me to liberty,
And enable me so to live now
That I may answer before you and before me.
Lord, whatever this day may bring,
Your name be praised.

—DIETRICH BONHOEFFER

O Lord give me strength that the whole world look to me with the eyes of a friend. Let us ever examine each other with the eyes of a friend.

—YAYURVEDA

The most powerful prayer, one well nigh omnipotent, and the worthiest work of all is the outcome of a quiet mind.

—MEISTER ECKHART

God be in my head, and in my understanding;
God be in my eyes, and in my looking;
God be in my mouth, and in my speaking;
God be in my heart, and in my thinking;
God be at my end, and at my departing.

—SARUM PRIMER

Blessèd sister, holy mother, spirit of the
    fountain, spirit of the garden,
Suffer us not to mock ourselves with falsehood
Teach us to care and not to care
Teach us to sit still
Even among these rocks,
Our peace in His will
And even among these rocks
Sister, mother,
And spirit of the river, spirit of the sea,
Suffer me not to be separated

And let my cry come unto Thee.

—T.S. ELIOT
"Ash Wednesday"

*D*ear Pan, and all you other gods who live here, grant that I may become beautiful within, and that whatever outward things I have may be in harmony with the spirit inside me. May I understand that it is only the wise who are rich, and may I have only as much money as a temperate person needs. —Is there anything else that we can ask for, Phaedrus? For me, that prayer is enough.

—SOCRATES

If I had influence with the good fairy who is supposed to preside over the christening of all children, I should ask that her gift to each child in the world be a sense of wonder so indestructible that it would last throughout life.

—RACHEL CARSON

*O*Lord I ask you
In the name of Muhammad and his
  line of Progeny
To have Mercy on Muhammad and
  his posterity.
And (through them) grant me (also)
The light in my eyes, the true   .
  understanding of my faith

The (Divine) Certainty in my heart
The sincerity in my actions and
　　peace in my mind
And spaciousness in the means of
　　my living
And gratitude unto You
As long as you decide to keep me
　　alive.

—MUSLIM PRAYER
"Ayat-al-Kursi"

*O*nly a brief sleep everywhere
In man, in the green, in the cup of the winds.
Everyone goes home to his dead heart.

—I wish the world were still a child—
And was able to tell me how it first drew breath.

One time there was great piety in heaven;
The stars passed the Bible around to read.
If only I could take God's hand sometime
Or see on his finger the spinning moon.

O God, O God, how far I am from you!

—ELSE LASKER-SCHULER

*S*oul of Christ, sanctify me.
Body of Christ, save me.
Blood of Christ, inebriate me.
Water from the side of Christ, wash me.
Passion of Christ, strengthen me.
O good Jesus, hear me.
Within thy wounds hide me.
Permit me not to be separated from thee.
From the wicked foe defend me.
At the hour of my death call me
And bid me come to thee.
That with thy saints I may praise thee
For ever and ever.

—MEDIEVAL PRAYER
"Anima Christi"

Oh Lord,
Oh, my Lord,
Oh, my good Lord,
Keep me from sinking down.

I tell you what I mean to do,
Keep me from sinking down,
I mean to go to heaven too;
Keep me from sinking down.

—ANON
"Keep Me from Sinking Down"

*I*n itself, prayer is simply
reverent, conscious openness
to God full of the desire to
grow in goodness and
overcome evil.

—WILLIAM JOHNSTON

be generous.

u deserve;

ost;

the wounds;

to seek reward,

at of knowing that

do Your will, O God.

—St. Ignatius Loyola

*F*rom the cowardice t
face new truth
From the laziness that is contented
with half truth
From the arrogance that thinks it
knows all truth,
Good Lord, deliver me.

—KENYAN PRAYER

I now leave, not knowing when or whether ever I may return, with a task before me greater than that which rested upon Washington. Without the assistance of that Divine Being who ever attended him, I cannot succeed. With that assistance I cannot fail. Trusting in Him who can go with me, and remain with you, and be everywhere for good, let us confidently hope that all will yet be well.

—ABRAHAM LINCOLN
Farewell Address at Springfield
February 11, 1861

*T*his is our hope, this is the faith that I go back South with.

With this faith we will be able to hew out of the mountain of despair a stone of hope. With this faith we will be able to transform the jangling discords of our nation into a beautiful symphony of brotherhood.

With this faith we will be able to work together, to pray together, to struggle together, to go to jail together, to stand up for freedom together, knowing that we will be free one day. . . .

—MARTIN LUTHER KING, JR.
Speech at the Lincoln Memorial
August 28, 1963

...we ought to have
...d have not thought,
All that we ought to have said, and
  have not said,
All that we ought to have done, and
  have not done;

All that we ought not to have
  thought, and yet have thought,
All that we ought not to have
  spoken, and yet have spoken,

All that we ought not to have done,
   and yet have done;
For thoughts, words and works,
   pray we, O God, for forgiveness.

—PERSIAN PRAYER

𝓑atter my heart, three-person'd God; for you
As yet but knock, breathe, shine, and seek
    to mend;
That I may rise, and stand, o'erthrow me,
    and bend
Your force, to break, blow, burn and make
    me new.
I, like an usurp'd town, to another due,
Labour to admit you, but Oh, to no end,
Reason your viceroy in me, me should defend,
But is captiv'd, and proves weak or untrue.

Yet dearly I love you, and would be loved fain,
But am betroth'd unto your enemy:
Divorce me, untie, or break that knot again,
Take me to you, imprison me, for I
Except you enthral me, never shall be free,
Nor ever chaste, except you ravish me.

—JOHN DONNE
"Sonnet XIV"

$\mathcal{I}$ come before thee as one of thy many
children. See, I am small and weak; I need
thy strength and wisdom.

Grant me to walk in beauty and that my eyes
may ever behold the crimson sunset. May
my hands treat with respect the things
which thou hast created, may my ears hear
thy voice!

Make me wise, that I may understand the
things which thou hast taught my people,
which thou hast hidden in every leaf and
every rock.

I long for strength, not in order that I may
overreach my brother but to fight my
greatest enemy—myself.
Make me ever ready to come to thee with pure
hands and candid eyes, so that my spirit,
when life disappears like the setting sun,
may stand unashamed before thee.

—SIOUX PRAYER

*G*reat Spirit, Great Spirit, my Grandfather,
all over the earth the faces of living things are
    all alike.
With tenderness have these come up out of the
    ground.
Look upon these faces of children without
    number
and with children in their arms,
that they may face the winds
and walk the good road to the day of quiet.

—BLACK ELK

*N*ow I lay me down to sleep,
I pray the Lord my soul to keep;
If I should die before I wake,
I pray the Lord my soul to take.

—A Child's Evening Prayer

Cold, slow, silent, but returning,
  after so many hours.
The sight of something outside me,
  the day is breaking.
May salt, this one day, be sharp
  upon my tongue;
May I sleep, this one night, without
  waking.

—RANDALL JARRELL
"A Prayer at Morning"

Lord, I believe;
help thou mine unbelief.

—MARK 9:24

My Lord, I do not believe.
Help thou mine unbelief.

—SAMUEL BUTLER

Wild Nights—Wild Nights!
Were I with thee
Wild Nights should be
Our luxury!

Futile—the Winds—
To a Heart in port—
Done with the Compass—
Done with the Chart!

Rowing in Eden—
Ah, the Sea!
Might I but moor—Tonight—
In Thee!

—EMILY DICKINSON

*L*ord, kind today but brutal
   yesterday,
Lord of two faces—vengefulness and
   love—
I toss you, just like dice tossed in
   the wind,
my prayer of blasphemy and praise!

—ANTONIO MACHADO
"The Iberian God"

*O*pen your doors to us, O Lord.
The day goes down; the sun falls,
the sun disappears. Eternal, we
come to your doors. We implore
you: Pardon us. We implore you:
Have mercy upon us. Save us!

—NIKOS KAZANTZAKIS
The Last Temptation of Christ

The noblest prayer is that,
when he who prays
Is inwardly transformed to
that he kneels before.

—Angelus Silesius

*G*od, I offer myself to Thee—to build with me and to do with me as Thou wilt. Relieve me of the bondage of self, that I may better do Thy will. Take away my difficulties, that victory over them may bear witness to those I would help of Thy Power, Thy Love, and Thy Way of life. May I do Thy will always!

—ALCOHOLICS ANONYMOUS

O Lord Jesus Christ
who art as the shadow of a great rock in a
    weary land,
who beholdest thy weak creatures
weary of labour, weary of pleasure,
weary of hope deferred, weary of self,
in thine abundant compassion,
and fellow feeling with us,
and unutterable tenderness,
bring us we pray thee,
unto thy rest.

—CHRISTINA ROSSETTI
"In Weariness"

O Savior, as thou hang'st upon the tree;
I turn my back to thee, but to receive
Corrections, till thy mercies bid thee leave.
O think me worth thine anger, punish me,
Burn off my rusts, and my deformity,
Restore thine image, so much, by thy grace,
That thou may'st know me, and I'll turn my
    face.

—JOHN DONNE
"Good Friday, 1613. Riding Westward."

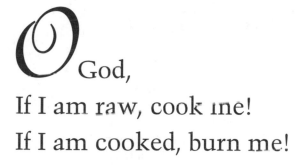

O God,
If I am raw, cook me!
If I am cooked, burn me!

—Kwaja Abdullah Ansari

Lord, let Your light be only for the day,
And the darkness for the night.
And let my dress, my poor humble dress
Lie quietly over my chair at night.

Let the church-bells be silent,
My neighbour Ivan not ring them at night.
Let the wind not waken the children
Out of their sleep at night.

Let the hen sleep on its roost, the horse in the stable
All through the night.
Remove the stone from the middle of the road
That the thief may not stumble at night.

Let heaven be quiet during the night,
Restrain the lightning, silence the thunder,
They should not frighten mothers giving birth
To their babies at night.

And me too protect against fire and water,
Protect my poor roof at night.
Let my dress, my poor humble dress
Lie quietly over my chair at night.

—NECHUM BRONZE

𝓛ord, in your great generosity,
heal my sickness, wash away my defilement,
enlighten my blindness, enrich my poverty,
and clothe my nakedness.
May I receive the bread of angels,
the King of kings and Lord of lords,
with humble reverence,
with the purity and faith,
the repentance and love, and the determined
    purpose
that will help to bring me to salvation.

—St. Thomas Aquinas

The long days of our sorrow still endure;
Father, grant to the soul thou hast been
    chastening
that thou hast promised, the healing and the
    cure.
Should it be ours to drain the cup of grieving
even to the dregs of pain, at thy command,
we will not falter, thankfully receiving
all that is given by thy loving hand.

—DIETRICH BONHOEFFER

O Lord!
thou knowest how busy
I must be this day:
if I forget thee,
do not thou forget me.

—SIR JACOB ASTLEY

*L*ord, hear me out,
and hear me out this
    day:
From me to Thee's
    a long and terrible way.

—THEODORE ROETHKE

At Tara today in this fateful
  hour
I place all heaven with its power,
And the sun with its brightness,
And the snow with its whiteness,
And fire with all the strength it
  has,
And lightning with its rapid wrath
And the winds with their swiftness
  along the path,

And the sea with its deepness,
And the rocks with their steepness
And the Earth with its starkness,
All these I place
By God's almighty help and grace,
Between myself and the powers of
   Darkness.

—St. Patrick

Thou, my Lord Jesus Christ, Thou who camest into the world in order to save those who were lost, Thou who didst leave the ninety and nine sheep in order to look for the lost one, look Thou for me in the path of my errors, where I hide myself from Thee and from mankind. Thou the good shepherd let me hear Thy gentle voice, let me know it, let me follow it!

—SØREN KIERKEGAARD

*W*a-kon'da,
here needy he stands,
and I am he.

—OMAHA TRIBAL PRAYER

If the love You have for me
Is like the love I have for You,
My God, what detains me?
Oh, what is delaying You?

—ST. TERESA OF AVILA

O God who made this beautiful earth, when will it be ready to receive your saints? How long, O Lord, how long?

—George Bernard Shaw

I call to Nature, the mother of all, the mother
    who makes,
Heavenly, honored, goddess of wealth, sovereign,
The one who wins, who is never tamed, the narrator,
    the Giver of Light,
Stronger than the strongest, who gives her breasts to
    all,
Who never dies, the firstborn, known in legends,
    who helps us do,
Born of the night, all wisdom, carrier of light, a
    strong holder-back,
We see your footprints that whirl silently when you
    are still.

—ORPHIC HYMN

*G*od guard me from those thoughts men think
In the mind alone;
He that sings a lasting song
Thinks in a marrow-bone;

From all that makes a wise old man
That can be praised of all;
O what am I that I should not seem
For the song's sake a fool?

I pray—for fashion's word is out
And prayer comes round again—
That I may seem, though I die old,
A foolish, passionate man.

—WILLIAM BUTLER YEATS
"A Prayer for Old Age"

n the sun even

not shining.

I believe in love even when

feeling it not.

I believe in God even when

he is silent.

—JEWISH PRAYER

*A*bsolute attention is
prayer.

—ZEN SAYING

`My Lord God, I have no idea where I am going. I do not see the road ahead of me. I cannot know for certain where it will end. Nor do I really know myself and the fact that I think that I am following Your will does not mean that I am actually doing so. But I believe that the desire to please You does in fact please You. And I hope that I have that desire in all that I am doing. I hope that I will never do anything apart from that desire. And I know

that if I do this, You will lead me by the right
road though I may know nothing about it.
Therefore will I trust You always though I may
seem to be lost and in the shadow of death. I
will not fear, for You are ever with me, and You
will never leave me to face my perils alone.

—THOMAS MERTON

The way I must enter
leads through darkness to
   darkness—
O moon above the mountains' rim,
please shine a little further
on my path.

—Izumi Shikibu

*O*shooting star
that fell into my eyes and
   through my body—:
Not to forget you. To endure.

—RAINER MARIA RILKE
"Death"

$\mathcal{G}$od of our life,
there are days when the burdens we carry
chafe our shoulders and weigh us down;
when the road seems dreary and endless,
the skies gray and threatening;
when our lives have no music in them,
and our hearts are lonely,
and our souls have lost their courage.
Flood the path with light,
run our eyes to where
the skies are full of promise;

tune our hearts to brave music;
give us the sense of comradeship
with heroes and saints of every age;
and so quicken our spirits
that we may be able to encourage
the souls of all who journey with us
on the road of life, to your honor and glory.

—St. Augustine

*G*od grant me the
serenity to accept the things I
   cannot change;
courage to change the things I can;
and wisdom to know the difference.

Living one day at a time;
Enjoying one moment at a time;
Accepting hardships as the pathway
   to peace;

Taking this sinful world as it is,
  not as I would have it;
Trusting that you will make all
  things right if I surrender
    to your will;
That I may be reasonably happy in
  this life
And supremely happy with you
  forever in the next.

—ATTRIBUTED TO REINHOLD NIEBUHR

Beloved, let us love one another: for love is of God; and every one that loveth is born of God, and knoweth God. He that loveth not knoweth not God; for God is love.

—1 JOHN 4:7

Almighty and everlasting God, who art always more ready to hear than we to pray, and art wont to give more than either we desire, or deserve: Pour down upon us the abundance of thy mercy; forgiving us those things whereof our conscience is afraid, and giving us those good things which we are not worthy to ask, but through the merits and mediation of Jesus Christ, thy Son, our Lord. Amen.

—THE BOOK OF COMMON PRAYER

Silent friend of many distances, feel
how your breath enlarges all of space.
Let your presence ring out like a bell
into the night. What feeds upon your face

grows mighty from the nourishment thus
offered. Move through transformation, out and
in. What is the deepest loss that you have
suffered? If drinking is bitter, change yourself to
wine.

In this immeasurable darkness, be the power
that rounds your senses in their magic ring,
the sense of their mysterious encounter.

And if the earthly no longer knows your name,
whisper to the silent earth: I'm flowing.
To the flashing water say: I am.

—RAINER MARIA RILKE
The Sonnets to Orpheus

We wait in the darkness!
  Come, all ye who listen,
    Help in our night journey:
    Now no sun is shining;
    Now no star is glowing;
    Come show us the pathway:
    The night is not friendly;
  The moon has forgot us,
We wait in the darkness!

—IROQUOIS PRAYER

*H*ow many nights
have I lain in terror,
O Creator Spirit, Maker of night and day,

only to walk out
the next morning over the frozen world
hearing under the creaking of snow
faint, peaceful breaths . . .
snake,
bear, earthworm, ant . . .

and above me
a wild crow crying *'yaw yaw yaw'*
from a branch nothing cried from ever in my life.

—GALWAY KINNELL
"How Many Nights"

I know that thou canst do every thing, and that no thought can be withholden from thee.

Who is he that hideth counsel without knowledge? therefore have I uttered that I understood not; things too wonderful for me, which I knew not.

Hear, I beseech thee, and I will speak: I will demand of thee, and declare thou unto me.

I have heard of thee by the hearing of the ear: but now mine eye seeth thee.

Wherefore I abhor myself, and repent in dust and ashes.

—JOB 42:2–6

*W*hat does it matter how I pray, so long as my prayers are answered?

—SITTING BULL

Raise me up, Lord, who am fallen down,
void of love and fear and faith and awe;
I long to rise and in my place abide;
mine is the longing, mine the impediment.

Between thy might and mercy I am torn;
in others every day I see amend,
in me I see fresh longing to offend thee.

—MIGUEL DE GUEVARA
"Raise Me Up, Lord"

I am here abroad,
I am here in need,
I am here in pain,
I am here in straits,
I am here alone.
O God, aid me.

—CELTIC CHARM

*G*randfather,
Look at our brokenness.

We know that in all creation
Only the human family
Has strayed from the Sacred Way.

We know that we are the ones
Who are divided
And we are the ones
Who must come back together
To walk in the Sacred Way.

Grandfather,
Sacred One,
Teach us love, compassion, and honor
That we may heal the earth
And heal each other.

—OJIBWA PRAYER

*M*y Lord and my Creator,
you bear with me and nourish me—
   be my helper.
I thirst for you, I hunger for you, I desire you,
   I sigh for you, I covet you:
I am like an orphan deprived of the presence
   of a very kind father,
who, weeping and wailing, does not cease to cling to
   the dear face with his whole heart.
I want you, I hope for you, I seek you;
'to you my heart has said, seek my face';
'your face, Lord, have I sought;
   turn not your face from me.'

—St. Anselm

Wilt Thou forgive that sin where I begun,
   Which is my sin, though it were done before?
Wilt Thou forgive that sin, through which I run,
   And do run still: though still I do deplore?
      When Thou hast done, Thou has not done,
         For, I have more.

—JOHN DONNE
"A Hymn to God the Father"

$\mathcal{I}$f anyone has hurt me or harmed me
knowingly or unknowingly in thought, word, or
deed, I freely forgive them.

And I too ask forgiveness if I have hurt
anyone or harmed anyone knowingly or
unknowingly in thought, word, or deed.

> May I be happy
> May I be peaceful
> May I be free
>
> May my friends be happy
> May my friends be peaceful
> May my friends be free

May my enemies be happy
May my enemies be peaceful
May my enemies be free

May all things be happy
May all things be peaceful
May all things be free.

—BUDDHIST PRAYER

*H*ear my prayer, O LORD, and let
my cry come unto thee.
Hide not thy face from me in the
day when I am in trouble; incline
thine ear unto me: in the day
when I call answer me speedily.
My days are like a shadow that
declineth; and I am withered like
grass.

—PSALM 102:1–2, 11

Out of the depths have I cried unto thee, O Lord.

Lord, hear my voice: let thine ears be attentive to the voice of my supplications.

If thou, Lord, shouldest mark iniquities, O Lord, who shall stand?

But there is forgiveness with thee, that thou mayest be feared.

I wait for the Lord, my soul doth wait, and in his word do I hope.

My soul waiteth for the Lord more than they that watch for the morning: I say, more than they that watch for the morning.

Let Israel hope in the Lord: for with the Lord there is mercy, and with him is plenteous redemption.

And he shall redeem Israel from all his iniquities.

—Psalm 130

This time, I have left my body behind me,
    crying
In its dark thorns.
Still,
There are good things in this world.
It is dusk.
It is the good darkness
Of women's hands that touch loaves.
The spirit of a tree begins to move.
I touch leaves.
I close my eyes, and think of water.

—JAMES WRIGHT
"Trying to Pray"

In a corrupt age,
when prayers are not
answered,
that itself is the answer.

—MUSO KOKUSHI

There is nothing I can give you Which you do not have; but there is much, very much, that while I cannot give it, you can take.

No heaven can come to us unless our hearts find rest in today. Take heaven! No peace lies in the future which is not hidden in this present instant. Take peace!

The gloom of the world is but a
shadow. Behind it, yet within reach,
is joy. There is radiance and glory
in the darkness, could we but see,
and to see, we have only to look. I
beseech you to look

—FRA GIOVANNI

*A*nd Jesus saith to his disciples, "Sit ye here, while I shall pray." And he went forward a little, and fell on the ground, and prayed that, if it were possible, the hour might pass from him.

And he said, "Ab'-ba, Father, all things are possible unto thee; take away this cup from me: nevertheless not what I will, but what thou wilt."

—MARK 14:32b, 35–36

J am not eager, bold
Or strong—all that is past.
I am ready not to do,
At last, at last!

—St. Peter Canisius

Bow, stubborn knees!

—William Shakespeare
Hamlet

Your prayer should be, "Break
  the legs
of what I want to happen.
  Humiliate
my desire. Eat me like candy.
It's spring, and finally
I have no will."

—JELALUDDIN RUMI

*Y*ou hear the long roll of the plunging ground,
The whistle of stones, the quail's cry in the
   grass.
I stammer like a bird, I rasp like stone,
I mutter, with gray hands upon my face.
The earth blurs, beyond me, into dark.
Spinning in such bewildered sleep, I need
To know you, whirring above me, when I wake.
Come down. Come down. I lie afraid.
I have lain alien in my self so long,
How can I understand love's angry tongue?

—JAMES WRIGHT
"A Prayer in My Sickness"

There is no life with[out]
prayer. Without prayer [there]
is only madness and h[orror.]

—Vas[...]

ve

out

there

rror.

a foundation

l death.

ed into a

, which will

LI ROZANOV

and yet,

return again.

—ANNE FRANK

Deliver me from my own shadows, my Lord, from the wrecks and confusion of my days.

—RABINDRANATH TAGORE

To God: to illuminate all men. Beginning with Skid Road.

Let Occidental and Washington be transformed into a higher place, the plaza of eternity.

Illuminate the welders in shipyards with the brilliance of their torches.

Let the crane operator lift up his arm for joy.

Let elevators creak and speak, ascending and descending in awe.

Let the mercy of the flower's direction beckon in the eye.

Let the straight flower bespeak its purpose in
straightness—to seek the light.

Let the crooked flower bespeak its purpose in
crookedness—to seek the light.

Let the crookedness and straightness bespeak the
light.

Let Puget Sound be a blast of light.

I feed on your Name like a cockroach on a
crumb—this cockroach is holy.

—ALLEN GINSBERG
"Psalm III"

*L*isten
with the night falling we are saying thank you
we are stopping on the bridges to bow from the railings
we are running out of the glass rooms
with our mouths full of food to look at the sky
and say thank you
we are standing by the water looking out
in different directions

back from a series of hospitals back from a mugging
after funerals we are saying thank you
after the news of the dead
whether or not we knew them we are saying thank you
looking up from tables we are saying thank you
in a culture up to its chin in shame
living in the stench it has chosen we are saying thank you

over telephones we are saying thank you
in doorways and in the backs of cars and in elevators
remembering wars and the police at the back door
and the beatings on stairs we are saying thank you
in the banks that use us we are saying thank you
with the crooks in office with the rich and fashionable
unchanged we go on saying thank you thank you

with the animals dying around us
our lost feelings we are saying thank you
with the forests falling faster than the minutes
of our lives we are saying thank you
with the words going out like cells of a brain
with the cities growing over us like the earth
we are saying thank you faster and faster
with nobody listening we are saying thank you
we are saying thank you and waving
dark though it is

—W.S. MERWIN

$\mathcal{M}$other of gods, father of gods,
Ancient God,
A mere appendage of the realm, a
common man, has come.
He comes crying, he comes in
sadness, he comes with guilt.
Perhaps he has slipped, perhaps he
has stumbled, perhaps he has
touched the bird of evil, the
spider's web, the tuft of thorns:

It wounds his heart, it troubles
    him.
Master, Lord,
Ever Present, Ever Near,
Take it from him: hear the pain of
    this common man.

—AZTEC PRAYER

The Road goes ever on and on
   Down from the door where it began.
Now far ahead the Road has gone,
   And I must follow, if I can,
Pursuing it with eager feet,
   Until it joins some larger way
Where many paths and errands meet.
   And whither then? I cannot say.

—J.R.R. TOLKIEN

$\mathcal{S}$unset and evening sta
    And one clear call for
And may there be no mo
    When I put out to sea.

———◆———

For though from out our bourne of time and place
    The flood may bear me far,
I hope to see my pilot face to face
    When I have crossed the bar.

—ALFRED, LORD TENNYSON
"Crossing the Bar"

...l to you gods . . .
    ...hat day of the great reckoning.
    ...hold me, I have come to you,
Without sin, without guilt, without evil,
Without a witness against me,
Without one whom I have wronged. . . .
Rescue me, protect me,
Do not accuse me before the great god!

I am one pure of mouth, pure of hands.

—THE BOOK OF THE DEAD

*S*ometimes a man stands up during supper and walks outdoors, and keeps on walking, because of a church that stands somewhere in the East.

And his children say blessings on him as if he were dead.

And another man, who remains inside his own house, stays there, inside the dishes and in the glasses, so that his children have to go far out into the world toward that same church, which he forgot.

—RAINER MARIA RILKE

*A*bide with me: fast falls the
  eventide;
The darkness deepens; Lord, with
  me abide;
When other helpers fail, and
  comforts flee,
Help of the helpless, O abide with
  me.

—HENRY FRANCIS LYTE
"Eventide"

I have gone forward with
Some, a few lonely some.
They have fallen to death.
I die with them.
Lord, I have loved Thy cursed,
The beauty of Thy house:
Come down. Come down. Why dost
Thou hide thy face?

—JAMES WRIGHT
"Speak"

*A*t a certain point you say to the woods, to the sea, to the mountains, the world, Now I am ready. Now I will stop and be wholly attentive. You empty yourself and wait, listening. After a time you hear it: there is nothing there. There is nothing but those things only, those created objects, discrete, growing or holding, or swaying, being rained on or raining, held, flooding or ebbing, standing, or spread. You feel the world's word as a tension, a hum, a single chorused note everywhere the same. This is it: this hum is the silence.

———◆———

The silence is all there is. It is the alpha and the omega. It is God's brooding over the face of the waters; it is the blended note of the ten thousand things, the whine of wings. You take a step in the right direction to pray to this silence, and even to address the prayer to "World." Distinctions blur. Quit your tents. Pray without ceasing.

—ANNIE DILLARD

*H*ow many nights must it take
one such as me to learn
that we aren't, after all, made
from that bird which flies out of its ashes,
that for a man
as he goes up in flames, his one work
is
to open himself, to *be*
the flames?

—GALWAY KINNELL

O God, the night has passed and the day
dawned. How I long to know if Thou hast
accepted my prayers or if Thou hast rejected
them. Therefore console me for it is Thine to
console this state of mine. Thou hast given me
life and cared for me, and Thine is the glory. If
Thou want to drive me from Thy door, yet
would I not forsake it, for the love that I bear in
my heart towards Thee.

—RABI'A

mid the encircling

...nd I am far from home,
...e on.
...ep thou my feet; I do not ask to see
The distant scene; one step enough for me.

I was not ever thus, nor prayed that thou
Shouldst lead me on;
I loved to choose and see my path; but now
Lead thou me on.
I loved the garish day, and, spite of fears,
Pride ruled my will: remember not past years.

So long thy power hath blest me, sure it still
Will lead me on
O'er moor and fen, o'er crag and torrent, till
The night is gone,
And with the morn those Angel faces smile,
Which I have loved long since, and lost awhile.

—JOHN HENRY NEWMAN
"Lead, Kindly Light"

When the spent sun throws up its rays on
   cloud
And goes down burning into the gulf below,
No voice in nature is heard to cry aloud
At what has happened. Birds, at least, must
   know
It is the change to darkness in the sky.
Murmuring something quiet in her breast,
One bird begins to close a faded eye;
Or overtaken too far from his nest,
Hurrying low above the grove, some waif
Swoops just in time to his remembered tree.

At most he thinks or twitters softly, "Safe!
Now let the night be dark for all of me.
Let the night be too dark for me to see
Into the future. Let what will be, be."

—ROBERT FROST
"Acceptance"

I want to die easy when I
die.
I want to die easy when I die.
Shout salvation as I fly,
I want to die easy when I die.

—AFRICAN-AMERICAN SPIRITUAL

*M*ay the Father take you
In his fragrant clasp of love,
When you go across the
   flooding streams
And the black river of death.

—CELTIC BLESSING

*W*hen the signs of age begin to mark my
    body
(and still more when they touch my mind);
when the ill that is to diminish me or carry me
    off strikes from without
or is born within me;
when the painful moment comes in which I
    suddenly waken
to the fact that I am ill or growing old;
and above all at the last moment
when I feel I am losing hold of myself
and am absolutely passive in the hands

of the great unknown forces that have formed
    me;
in all those dark moments, O God,
grant that I may understand that it is you
(provided only my faith is strong enough)
who are painfully parting the fibers of my being
in order to penetrate to the very marrow of my
    substance
and bear me away within yourself.

—TEILHARD DE CHARDIN

Grandfather, Great Father, let matters go well with me, for I am going into the forest.

—BAMBUTI PYGMY PRAYER

*I*f a dead person were allowed to return to this world and pray, you can be sure that he would pray with all his might.

—RABBI NACHMAN OF BRATSLO

From delusion lead me to
  Truth.
From darkness lead me to
  Light.
From death lead me to
  Immortality.

—THE UPANISHADS

*L*ord! can't you see I'm weary
Of this rising and dying and living.
Take it all, but once more bring me
   close
To sense the freshness of this
   crimson rose.

—ANNA AKHMATOVA
"Last Rose"

*A*nd if tonight my soul may find
   her peace
in sleep, and sink in good oblivion,
and in the morning wake like a
   new-opened flower
then I have been dipped again in
   God, and new-created.

—D.H. LAWRENCE

*G*od bless us every one!

—CHARLES DICKENS
"Tiny Tim's Prayer"

A Selective Guide

$\mathcal{F}$or those who wish, we offer the following highly selective list of prayers, arranged by topic, time of day, or particular need. Of course, the interpretation of prayer is very personal, so please view this guide only as a starting point.

AWE & WONDER 18, 50, 68, 72, 145, 156, 184

BENEDICTIONS & BLESSINGS 124, 135, 181, 212, 220, 265, 282

CONTRITION & SORROW 216, 231, 252, 278, 280, 302

DAILY PRAYERS
MORNING: 75, 128, 152, 196, 236, 284
DAYTIME: 38, 141, 229, 299
EVENING: 12, 54, 142, 288, 358
NIGHT: 127, 129, 244, 294, 322

INDEX

Asterisked page numbers indicate the ABOUT PRAYER features.

ACKNOWLEDGMENTS

We gratefully acknowledge the following for permission to reprint material copyrighted or controlled by them. Every effort has been made to clear reprints. If any required credits have been omitted or any rights overlooked, it is completely unintentional, and we will gladly correct any omissions in future reprints.

◆Excerpt from p. 63 of *Alcoholics Anonymous*. Reprinted with permission. ◆Lyrics from "Father of Night" by Bob Dylan. Copyright © 1970 by Big Sky Music. All rights reserved. International copyright secured. Used by permission. ◆"Owning Everything" written by Leonard Cohen. Copyright © 1961 by Leonard Cohen. Used by permission. All rights reserved. ◆"Human Wisdom" by Charles Peguy from *Short Prayers for the Long Day*, compiled by Giles & Melville Harcourt. Published by Collins, 1978. ◆"Song to the Creator" by St. Hildegard of Bingen. Reprinted from *St. Hildegard of Bingen: Symposia, A Critical Edition of the Symphonia armonie celestium revelationum*, ed./transl. Barbara Newman. Copyright © 1989 by Cornell University. By permission of the publisher, Cornell University Press. ◆Excerpts from *Celtic Prayer*, transl. Alexander Carmichael, ed. Trace Murphy. An Image Book published by Doubleday, a division of Bantam Doubleday Dell Publishing Group, Inc., 1996. ◆Lines from "The Marrow" from *The Collected Works of Theodore Roethke* by Theodore Roethke. Copyright © 1964 by Beatrice Roethke, Administratrix of the Estate of Theodore Roethke. By permission of Doubleday, a division of Bantam Doubleday Dell Publishing Group, Inc., and Faber and Faber, Ltd. ◆Excerpt from *Goodnight Willie Lee, I'll See You in The Morning* by Alice Walker. Copyright © 1975 by Alice Walker. By permission of Doubleday, a division of Bantam Doubleday Dell Publishing Group, Inc., and Wendy Weil Agency. ◆Excerpt from "A Prayer at Morning" from *The Complete Poems* by Randall Jarrell. Copyright © 1969 by Mrs. Randall Jarrell. By permission of Farrar, Straus & Giroux and Faber and Faber, Ltd. ◆Excerpts from *Thoughts in Solitude* by Thomas Merton. Copyright © 1956, 1958 by the Abbey of Gethsemani, copyright renewed 1986. Published by Farrar, Straus & Giroux. Reprinted by permission. ◆Excerpts from *The World of Prayer, Vol. 1* by Rabbi Dr. Elie Monk. Philipp Feldheim, Inc., Publisher. ◆Excerpt of poem by Jelaluddin Rumi from *When Grapes Turn to Wine*, published by Firefly Books, Ltd. ◆Excerpt from "Ash Wednesday" in *Collected Poems 1909–1962* by T.S. Eliot, copyright © 1936 by Harcourt Brace & Co., copyright renewed 1963, 1964 by T.S. Eliot. By permission of the publisher and Faber and Faber, Ltd. ◆Excerpt from *The Color Purple* by Alice Walker. Copyright © 1982 by Alice Walker. By permission

ABOUT THE EDITOR

*D*avid Schiller is a writer who has found much beauty and consolation in the world's prayers. His most recent book was *The Little Zen Companion* (Workman). He and his family live in Montclair, New Jersey.